Twayne's United States Authors Series

Sylvia E. Bowman, *Editor*

INDIANA UNIVERSITY

Sherwood Bonner
(Catherine McDowell)

TUSAS 269

Sherwood Bonner

SHERWOOD BONNER
(CATHERINE McDOWELL)

By WILLIAM L. FRANK
Longwood College

TWAYNE PUBLISHERS
A DIVISION OF G. K. HALL & CO., BOSTON

Library of Congress Cataloging in Publication Data

Frank, William L
  Sherwood Bonner (Catherine McDowell)

  (Twayne's United States authors series; TUSAS 269)
  Bibliography: p. 153–56.
  Includes index.
  1. McDowell, Katherine Sherwood Bonner, 1849–1883.
I. Title.
PS2358.F7   813'.4   76-6900
ISBN 0-8057-7169-7

To my mother and father, who
first introduced me to books; to
Dan Young, who helped me to
appreciate them; and to my
wife, Angeline, who helps me to
find the time to enjoy them.

Contents

About the Author

William L. Frank, currently Professor of English and Chairman of the Department of English and Philosophy at Longwood College in Farmville, Virginia, was born in the Bronx, New York City. Educated in the parochial schools in New York, he entered the Air Force upon graduation from Cardinal Hayes High School, and served for four years, teaching in Radio Operating School. After he was discharged, he completed his B.A. and M.Ed. degrees at the University of Southern Mississippi, and received his M.A. and Ph.D. in English from Northwestern University. He was a teaching fellow at both schools, and he has also taught at Delta State University in Cleveland, Mississippi, and at Southeast Missouri State University in Cape Girardeau, Missouri.

He has published articles in *College English* and *Notes on Mississippi Writers*, and he is currently editing a collection of Sherwood Bonner's stories for the Masterworks of Literature Series, under the general editorship of William S. Osborne. Active in professional societies, Professor Frank is presently Secretary-Treasurer of the South Atlantic Association of Departments of English.

Preface

Catherine McDowell (Sherwood Bonner), one of the South's first women novelists and a local-color writer of some achievement, was born in the small north Mississippi community of Holly Springs on February 26, 1849. By the time of her death in 1883 at the age of thirty-four, she had published one novel, a serial novelette, and a sufficient number of short stories in such periodicals as *Lippincott's* and *Harper's Monthly* to justify a two-volume collection. Although her work has never received a thorough critical examination and has not been included until recently in anthologies, a casual reader of Bonner's writings readily discovers for himself certain characteristics of her work that have contributed to the development of American literature: the use of the framework of the tale-within-the-tale narrative; the use of Negro dialect; and the strong satiric strain that permeates much of her short fiction.

Although Joel Chandler Harris is credited with using the first successful Negro dialect for its humorous effect, Bonner was writing dialect stories for *Lippincott's Magazine* at least four years before Harris' first Uncle Remus story appeared in the *Constitution*.[1] Indeed, by the time Harris' first Negro dialect story appeared, Bonner had published a sufficient number of such stories for the collection, *Dialect Tales*, which appeared in 1883. The intent of this book is, therefore, to trace the significant influences on Bonner and her early work; to summarize her relatively brief career; to touch on those aspects of her work enumerated above that have an enduring quality; and, finally, to suggest her place in the history of American literature.

Although it is not possible to construct a detailed account of Sherwood Bonner's early years, it is possible to sketch the environmental background in which she grew up and to record the principal influences which directed and controlled her later work. The first chapter of this book combines the known facts of Bonner's childhood with the hints found in her autobiographical fiction in order to present as accurate a statement of her earliest years as can be made. In chapter 2, I have again drawn from her published writings, as well as from unpublished diaries, manuscripts, and letters, to provide a thorough study of her relationship with Henry Wadsworth Longfellow, her literary sponsor and adviser.[2] The first two chapters are, therefore, wholly biographical in content.

The fictional works of Sherwood Bonner are discussed in the next three chapters. I have chosen this method of presentation to allow me to discuss, for example, all of the "Gran'mammy" stories under a single heading, although they initially appeared in several publications over an eight-year period. This treatment of Bonner's work allows the reader to see the progression of Sherwood Bonner from a local-color writer to one more intensely aware of, concerned with, and interested in the then newly emerging Realism of the late nineteenth century. As Claude Simpson has written in his anthology, *The Local Colorists* (1960), "She writes with a minimum of condescension, a good ear for dialect, and an awareness of sentimental formulas at which she occasionally directs gentle ridicule. Although not a major writer, she grew steadily during her brief career and might have become a literary figure of importance had she not died of cancer at an early age."[3] In the concluding chapter, I suggest a tentative appraisal of Bonner and her work, and show her as a minor but noteworthy transitional writer between the schools of Local Color and Realism.

In addition to her published fiction, Bonner traveled extensively and contributed numerous travel sketches and profiles of famous writers of the day, usually through serializations in the monthly magazines or in the weekly newspapers. These are discussed briefly in the early biographical chapters, for they have little literary merit. As to her poetry, Sherwood Bonner was only incidentally a poet. Although a recent bibliography lists over a dozen entries for her poetry, almost all the poems consist of only a few lines, frequently of nonsense verse, on a subject obviously directed toward very young children. Practically all of Bonner's poetry appears collected on a few pages in such publications as *Harper's Young People*. It is not, therefore, treated in this study.

WILLIAM L. FRANK

Longwood College

Acknowledgments

It is pleasurable to record the names of those to whom I am deeply indebted, for in recording them I also recall the pleasant associations connected with the preparation of this book. Thanks are due first to Professor Walter Rideout of the University of Wisconsin for suggesting a study of Bonner and to Professors Harrison Hayford and Ernest Samuels of Northwestern University for their advice and encouragement during the initial stages of this study. Were it not for the wholehearted cooperation of David McDowell of Batesville, Mississippi, and of Dr. George Stephenson of Jackson, Mississippi, the two surviving grand-nephews of Sherwood Bonner, I would not have had access to many unpublished letters and diaries now in their possession; I thank them most warmly for permission to use the primary material in their possession.

All biographers owe an enormous debt to their predecessors which they can never adequately acknowledge and to friends and colleagues. My thanks are due particularly to Nash Burger for his generous permission to use the materials he had accumulated for his master's thesis on Sherwood Bonner. I would also like to express my appreciation to Professors Peter Hilty of Southeast Missouri State University and Dan Young of Vanderbilt University, who read the manuscript in various stages of revision, and who made many fruitful suggestions regarding format and organization. Professors Wally Douglas of Northwestern University, H. O. Grauel of Southeast Missouri State University, and Phil Harth of the University of Wisconsin helped more than they will ever realize with counsel and encouragement at crucial times.

To Mrs. Janice Nunnelee of the Southeast Missouri State University library staff, I owe special thanks for locating and obtaining several nineteenth-century periodicals in which Sherwood Bonner had published. I would also like to express my appreciation to the following libraries which generously supplied me with copies of letters, stories, and manuscripts: the Cossitt Library of Memphis, Tennessee; the Duke University Library; the Houghton Library at Harvard University; the University of Missouri Library; the Lancaster Library of Longwood College; the University of Southern Mississippi Library; the Mississippi State University Library; and the State Archives Commission of Mississippi. I am also indebted to Miss Susan Davi and Mrs. Barbara Skerry of Longwood College for library assistance, and to Mrs. Henry Sessoms, Mrs. Janice Tinkle, and Mrs. Della Wickizer for clerical assistance.

Finally, I thank publicly and profusely my wife, Angeline, for serving as both mother and father to our children during much of the past two years, for transcribing Sherwood Bonner's *Diary* for the year 1869, and for willingly sharing me with Sherwood for the past several months.

Chronology

1849   Catherine Sherwood Bonner McDowell born, Holly Springs, Mississippi; oldest of three children.

1855   Enrolled in public school system of Holly Springs.

1858   Family moved into "Bonner House," large plantation home.

1859–   Attended Holly Springs Female Institute; excelled in Eng-
1861   lish composition.

1863   Attended Diocesan Female Seminary in Montgomery, Alabama.

1864   Published first short story in Boston *Ploughman*: "Laura Capello, A Leaf from a Traveler's Notebook."

1865   Death of mother, Mary Wilson Bonner.

1869   Published two short stories through efforts of Nahum Capen: "Italian Story" and "Marion's Mistake" (initial source unknown).

1871   Marriage to Edward McDowell, also of Holly Springs.

1872   Birth of only daughter, Lilian.

1873   Separation from husband; moved to Boston to earn her living by writing; wrote letter to H. W. Longfellow requesting an interview.

1875   Published first letter-article of a series in Memphis, Tennessee, *Avalanche*, May 4; launched her formal literary career with publication of first local-color story in *Youth's Companion*, July 29.

1875–   Served as Longfellow's amanuensis; assisted him in editing
1876   and compiling of *Poems of Places*.

1876   European travel, accompanied by Louise Chandler Moulton.

1878   Published only novel, *Like unto Like*, May 18; death of father and brother from yellow-fever plague in Holly Springs, September 7.

1880   Took up residence in Benton, Illinois, in order to establish residence for divorce from Edward; remained in Benton for fifteen months, from April, 1880 to July, 1881.

1881   Obtained final divorce decree and returned to Holly Springs in July; published "The Valcours" in four installments in *Lippincott's*, September through December.

1883   Published first of a two-volume collection of short stories, *Dialect Tales;* returned to Holly Springs knowing she was to die shortly; arrived in Holly Springs on March 7; died July 22.

1884   "Christmas Eve at Tuckeyho," published in *Lippincott's* in January; published "The Tender Conscience of Mr. Bobbert" in *Harper's Weekly* on March 22.

CHAPTER 1

The Formative Years

I General Influences of Time and Place

CATHERINE Sherwood Bonner McDowell was born February 26, 1849, in the north Mississippi community of Holly Springs.[1] Her parents were Southern planters, and during the early years of her life young Catherine experienced and enjoyed whatever material blessings could flow from the plantation system of the antebellum South. Her father, Dr. Charles Bonner, was born in County Antrim, Ireland, on October 28, 1814, of Scotch-Presbyterian parents.[2] While still a young boy, he came to the United States with his family; and they first settled in New York City but remained there less than a year. The family moved twice during the next four years, settling for a brief time in Penn Yan, New York, before moving permanently to Pennsylvania to work a "plantation of sugar maples that turned out to be hemlocks sold by a crooked speculator to the unsuspecting immigrants."[3]

The story of the hardships endured by the family reads like one of Hamlin Garland's accounts in *Main-Traveled Roads*. On this unpromising, wild, and for the most part unyielding soil, Charles Bonner's father sought "to work and develop the limited resources that were his."[4] The hard lot endured by Charles on this Pennsylvania farm did not dull either his sensibilities or his ambition. After earning his college degree, he continued his education and received a license to practice medicine.[5] Upon the receipt of his diploma from medical school, Charles decided to launch his professional career in what he felt was a more promising section of the country, and he thereupon headed for the South.[6] He practiced medicine briefly in the city of Huntsville, Alabama, before settling permanently in Holly Springs, Mississippi, shortly after the founding of the town in late 1835.[7] For the next twelve to fourteen years Dr. Bonner practiced his profession in this rapidly growing community which was referred to even in its earliest days as the capital of North Mississippi.

Although little is known about the courtship of Charles Bonner and Mary Wilson Bonner other than the fact that, as one family source states it, theirs was a "romantic courtship," some incidents described in Sherwood Bonner's autobiographical stories indicate that the marriage took place in 1847 or 1848. It would be difficult to imagine the marriage as occurring any earlier, for Mary Wilson, the mother of Sherwood Bonner, was born on May 5, 1828, of an aristocratic family that was not prone to encourage early marriage for its daughters.[8] At the same time, it is not very likely that the marriage could have taken place any later than 1848 since Sherwood was born in early 1849.

Mary Wilson, Dr. Bonner's fiancée, was of the Wilson-Davidson family that had come to Mississippi from Virginia through the Carolinas.[9] Her family was evidently quite wealthy, for the Wilson plantation in Holly Springs was one of the area's finest and most productive.[10] Whatever dowry Mary Wilson brought with her as the wife of Charles Bonner, it was sufficiently large to allow Dr. Bonner to retire from his medical practice immediately after his marriage, "dividing his time between the management of his estates, and the dispensing of an elegant hospitality in his home."[11] Although Dr. Bonner had been reared a Presbyterian, after his marriage to Mary Wilson he adopted the Episcopal religion of the Wilson family, and all of their children were reared in the Episcopal faith.

In spite of the fact that no record exists of the marriage between Charles Bonner and Mary Wilson, the affluence of the Wilson family is suggested in a description of the wedding feast recounted to Sherwood Bonner many years later by her Negro mammy. The description is found in one of Miss Bonner's earliest local-color stories, "The Night the Stars Fell":

'Jes' to think,' I heard gran'mammy say, 'at de housewarmin' when Miss Mary wus married, we wus one solid week a-bakin' and a-brewin', gittin' ready for de company. Dar wus poun'-cakes, as big roun' as barrel-tops; an' pigs, an' turkeys, an' chickens,—lor, you could n't begin to count 'em!

'An' as for de syllabub, an' custard, an' egg-nog, why dey wus jes' as common as water. Dat was a party wuth talkin' about.[12]

During the eighteen years of their marriage, Dr. and Mrs. Bonner had five children, only three of whom survived infancy. The first born was Catherine, christened Catherine Sherwood; the second, Ruth, was two years younger than Catherine, and she is portrayed in many of Sherwood Bonner's early dialect tales; and the last of the Bonner children to survive infancy was Samuel, five years Sherwood's junior, who, together with Dr. Bonner, was fatally stricken during the Yellow Fever epidemic of 1878.[13]

At the time of the marriage of Charles Bonner and Mary Wilson, the Bonner family owned few slaves. One, however, was Mary Wilson's Negro nurse, her Mammy, who rendered the same services for the Bonner children that she had for the Wilson children.[14] She accompanied Mary Wilson to Dr. Bonner's home; and, in the tradition of the family servants of the South in the midnineteenth century, she assumed the surname from the family she served. She appears in the Bonner family histories as "Gran'mammy," and she was more responsible than Sherwood's own mother for the rearing of the young Sherwood Bonner. Sherwood later presented her to the world as the central narrator-protagonist of at least half a dozen Negro dialect tales.

The relationship with Gran'mammy was only one of Sherwood Bonner's early experiences that influenced her literary career. Like most of the local-color writers, she was greatly affected by the physical environment in which she matured. As Sophia Kirk, Sherwood Bonner's closest friend during the last two years of her life has indicated, "Holly Springs, Mississippi, under one name or another, formed the scene of many of her stories."[15] Indeed, Holly Springs, usually only thinly disguised under such names as "Holly Well" or "Myrtle Springs," forms the setting for all but a few of Sherwood Bonner's stories. Since Miss Bonner was primarily interested in her early work in recreating the kind of society in which she herself grew up (a characteristic of the local-color school of fiction), it is important to indicate that, although the town of Holly Springs had itself been founded less than fifteen years before the birth of Sherwood Bonner, "a complete and typical specimen of the culture of the Old South" already existed in miniature in the community.

In the year 1850, only one year after the birth of Catherine Sherwood, Marshall County with 29,419 citizens was the most populous county in the state of Mississippi; and Holly Springs, its county seat with a population of 3,500, was one of the most prosperous cities in the state.[16] Between the Mexican War and the Civil War, Holly Springs prospered enormously. There soon appeared ornate man-sions and public buildings, the Mississippi Central Railroad, and an unusually comprehensive educational system for such a small community. Because of the phenomenal growth in population and in industry, Marshall County soon became known as the "Empire County."[17]

The city known today as Holly Springs came into existence as the rural settlement of Clarendon. The name was later changed to Paris, and finally, on April 4, 1836, the town was given its permanent name by William S. Randolph of Virginia, the founding father of Holly Springs.[18] By 1841, only five years after its founding, the population of Holly Springs totaled 1,117; and there were in operation nine dry-goods stores, five produce and grocery stores, one jewelry store, three hotels, six physicians' offices (including the one operated by Sherwood's father), fourteen law firms with a total of forty practicing attorneys, and five churches, including the Episcopal Church at which the Bonner family worshipped.[19]

The approximate time of Sherwood Bonner's birth also saw in Holly Springs the development of the Southern plantation home. One such home, built by a Mr. R. B. Alexander, an early settler, is described as a thirteen-room mansion "surrounded by flowers, grape arbors, a fish pond, an orchard, a private race track, a primitive cotton gin, the customary kitchen removed from the house, a separate smoke house, slave quarters, and other appurtenances of a prosperous plantation in the Old South."[20] Although no specific record exists of the plantation home into which Sherwood Bonner was born, the house built by her father shortly after her birth was similar in design and appearance to the Alexander home.

Of greater importance than these evidences of the material prosperity of the family and the region into which Sherwood Bonner was born, however, was the educational system of Holly Springs. It was, almost from its beginning, one of the most nearly complete in that area of the mid-South. As an early historian of Holly Springs has noted, "The history of the town of Holly Springs might be said to be the history of her educational endeavors, which have been notably successful. The educational field in which she most excelled had been the academy system which was so interwoven with life in the South before the Civil War."[21] The Bonner family itself was intimately connected with the educational enterprises of Holly Springs, for Sherwood's father served for a time as a member of the "Holly Springs Board of Trustees of the Public Schools of Holly Springs."

Moreover, Sherwood and her sister Ruth both attended the public-school system of that city.[22]

Since practically all of Sherwood's formal instruction was received in the Holly Springs school system, her later stories attest to the soundness of her early education. The strength of the educational system in turn was undoubtedly the result of the establishment and growth of Holly Springs' religious institutions. Less than five years after the founding of the town, the Presbyterians, Methodists, Baptists, and Episcopalians had not only church buildings with regularly scheduled services, but also pastors in residence, a unique situation for a community the size of Holly Springs in the 1840s.[23] These pastors were extremely active in initiating and encouraging the efforts of the citizens to build both public and private schools. The first school in Holly Springs was the Female Academy, authorized at a town meeting on August 24, 1836—the same year of the town's founding.[24]

A unique feature of this first school was that tuition fees were determined by one's scholastic distinction, and honor students received a kind of scholarship in the form of reduced tuition: first class tuition was eight dollars per semester; second class, twelve; and third class, fifteen.[25] In 1837, following the incorporation of the town of Holly Springs, fifty acres were set aside to construct a court house, a jail, and a new building for the Female Academy which was then utilizing a previously abandoned log building with a clapboard roof. An allocation from the county, coupled with a private subscription drive, produced slightly more than fourteen thousand dollars for the Academy.[26] In 1838, a classical school was established, and it had an enrollment of thirty-seven classical students and fifty-three English students. The following year the school was renamed, rather prematurely, the University of Holly Springs.[27]

Five years later, in January of 1844, and still five years before the birth of Sherwood Bonner, the Episcopal Church opened its first school, Saint Thomas Hall, which was reorganized as a military school in 1849.[28] In the same year, Franklin Female College was founded; and the school which Catherine Sherwood Bonner was later to attend, the Holly Springs Female Institute, was offering to its young ladies instruction in such courses as Ancient Languages, High Mathematics, Natural Sciences, Vocal and Instrumental Music, Chemistry, Higher English, the Evidences of Christianity, English Literature and Poetry, and Physiology and Hygiene.[29]

At the time of Sherwood Bonner's birth in 1849, therefore, Marshall County, of which Holly Springs was the county seat, could boast of three colleges with a combined faculty of thirteen teachers and a student enrollment of 250; thirteen public schools sustaining an enrollment of 380 pupils; and two academies having a combined faculty of fourteen teachers and a student body of 220.[30] Besides these formal areas of instruction, there were also available the tutorial services of traveling professional and resident semiprofessional teachers of foreign languages, English grammar, voice, piano, and violin.[31]

In addition to home and school life, the residents of Holly Springs had access to numerous cultural and recreational opportunities rarely found in small Southern communities. The principal entertainments offered, particularly to the young people, were the play and the public dinner which was invariably followed by a public dance. These dinners, given upon the slightest pretext, were always held upon the occasion of the visit of any person from outside Marshall County, whether the stranger was of national or merely of sectional note. At one such affair, thirteen separate toasts were offered, beginning with the traditional "To the Heroes of the Revolution," and concluding with the equally traditional "To the Ladies. In prosperity our purest source of pleasure, in adversity our best and truest friends."[32] On another such occasion a notice in one of the newspapers announced that "The celebrated Herr Schmidt gave a Grand Concert in the ball room . . . followed several days later with a Cotillion Party at Mr. Cate's Saloon."[33] That Sherwood herself attended such entertainments is indicated by a cursory perusal of her only existing diary that covers the year 1869, her twentieth year. In it, repeated references appear to her attendance at private and public dances and also at the frequently held community Philharmonic performances, for the young people of Holly Springs felt that these affairs constituted a part of their training in the social graces. Sherwood also alludes to such gatherings in many of her autobiographical works.

As entertaining as the public dinners and dances were to the citizens of Holly Springs, the play was probably the principal source of pleasure; for the drama afforded the young people opportunities to be both participants and spectators. Since Sherwood Bonner alludes throughout her diary to numerous theater parties, and since at

one point early in life she announces her decision "to be an actress
. . . after hesitating for a long time in favor of a literary life,"[34] one
may assume that the youthful Sherwood spent many of her leisure
hours attending the dramatic offerings of Holly Springs. But, despite popular appeal, the drama was not the only vehicle for culture
and entertainment in Holly Springs. Less than five years after the
founding of the city "The Holly Springs Library and Debating Society" was formed; and two years later a learned society called the
"Lyceum" was organized, members of which presented at each regular meeting papers on the arts, literature, and philosophy.[35] Sherwood Bonner's own interest in politics, illustrated by the central
conflict of her only published novel, might very well have been
stimulated by the activities of these two clubs. Although there is no
account of her attendance at a meeting of either of the two groups,
she does express throughout her 1869 diary a lively interest in the
politics of the day; and she records several instances in which she
and her acquaintances held lively political discussions.

In addition to the dramatic presentations, which afforded the
chief cultural recreation in Holly Springs, and to the intellectual and
philosophical discussion meetings, music also had its place in the
cultural pursuits of the citizens. There were several dancing schools
available to the young people of the city and ample opportunities to
take musical instruction. That music and dancing at private parties
played a large role in the lives of the young people is again evidenced by a careful reading of Sherwood Bonner's diary for the year
1869. Apart from the wedding parties described, generally elaborate
affairs with the music furnished by orchestras from Memphis, Tennessee, and not including the concerts and philharmonic presentations, Sherwood alludes to nineteen different "sociables" or home
entertainments that were usually given in honor of a departing
long-time resident, a visiting cousin, or a member of a traveling
professional troupe of some distinction.[36]

Together with the cultural and recreational offerings of Holly
Springs, still one other facet of life played an important role in
forming Bonner's personality—the hometown newspaper. In this
respect, too, Holly Springs appears to have been more fortunate
than many other towns twice its size; for a scant four years after its
founding the town could boast of three newspapers: the *Marshall
County Republican and Free Trade Advocate,* founded in August,

1838; the *Southern Banner*, which made its first appearance on January 18, 1839; and the *Southern Mercury*, the initial publication date of which is unknown.

These papers, issued either weekly or semiweekly, usually consisted of but four pages. The first page contained congressional reports; poetry, both local and national; stranger-than-fiction facts; and miscellaneous fillers, such as items of geography, population statistics, and the like. Pages two and three contained the local news, oftentimes largely social in nature and therefore of much interest to the younger set; political announcements—an entry by Sherwood in the diary for 1869 comments upon one such political announcement carried in the local press; letters to the editors; and the editorials. Page four was comprised largely of nonlocal advertisements (from which the more affluent young ladies ordered dress material), announcements of nonlocal cultural events, and occasionally notices of recently launched newspapers or periodicals seeking new subscribers.[37] Sherwood later utilized her familiarity with the local papers in obtaining a contract from the Memphis *Avalanche* for the publication of a series of travel sketches, the sale of which financed her European tour in 1876.

II *Specific Influence on Bonner's Later Work*

Despite the more than casual influence, however, of Holly Springs and its attractions upon the young Sherwood Bonner, there is no mistaking the three most important and enriching influences on the later local colorist. These three were the "Gran'mammy" figure, the Negro nurse that Sherwood was to "inherit" from her mother; her father's private library, housed in the spacious mansion known as "Bonner House"; and her schooling, brief as its formal nature was because of the intervention of the Civil War. Undoubtedly the strongest influence on the young child and growing girl was the Negro mammy who was later either the central figure or the narrator of many of Sherwood Bonner's Negro dialect tales. Gran'mammy was herself responsible for the origin of several of Bonner's tales; indeed, she narrated to the young Sherwood the story that Joel Chandler Harris immortalized three years later, "The Tar Baby." Gran'mammy delighted in an almost endless spinning of the sentimental and humorous folktales long associated with the earliest of the Southwest humorist, local-colorist tradition.

As one of Sherwood Bonner's early biographers has expressed it, "It was in the atmosphere of the maze of kettles, pothooks, long-handled waffle irons and frying pans made for the open hearth with its bed of hot coals that Katherine [*sic*] listened earnestly to the tales Gran'mammy told, tales that meant much more to the little girl than learning to sew."[38] Professor Alexander Bondurant, her earliest biographer, notes that "As a child she was fond of play, but she loved books and stories better still, and games ceased to charm, if Gran'mammy consented to tell her the story of the wonderful adventures of 'Brer Rabbit' and 'The Tar Baby,' or some of his other escapades, or if her papa came in bringing her a fresh volume of fairy stories."[39]

In her own writings Sherwood Bonner also recalls the nostalgic memories associated with Gran'mammy and her kitchen; for, as she writes in the Gran'mammy stories of *Suwanee River Tales*, "the great wide kitchen, with its roomy fire-place, where the backlog glowed and the black kettle swung, was the pleasantest place in the world."[40] Proof that Gran'mammy was in many respects a mother to the young Catherine is suggested in these same tales. It was "Gran'mammy to whom we ran to tell of triumphs and sorrows; she, whose sympathy, ash-cakes, and turnoverpies never failed us! It was she who hung over our sick-beds, who told us stories more beautiful than we read in any books; who sang to us old-fashioned hymns of praise and faith; and who talked to us with childlike simplicity of the God whom she loved."[41] Sherwood early acquired from careful attention to the tales told by Gran'mammy a fine ear for Negro dialect as well as a rich knowledge of Negro customs, religious practices, and superstitions—a knowledge that she used in many of her dialect and local-color stories.

The second most important influence on the young Sherwood Bonner was the accessibility and impressiveness of her father's library. The books were not only abundant but also carefully chosen. There were representative works of the English and classical writers that were so popular in the South of that era. A study of the literary allusions that occur in the published writings of Sherwood Bonner suggests that she first met some of these writers and works in her father's library during her youth in Holly Springs, and a close study of her only published novel reveals that such a premise is indeed valid. In *Like Unto Like*, when commenting upon the cultural in-

terests and literary pursuits of the citizens of Yariba (one of her
fictional names for Holly Springs), Bonner describes the principal
reading material usually found in the homes. As Professor Jay B.
Hubbell points out, one may assume that Bonner's own library in
Holly Springs contained such classics as she mentions in *Like Unto
Like*:[42]

Their reading was of a good, solid sort. They were brought up, as it were, as
Walter Scott. They read Richardson, and Fielding, and Smollett, though
you may be sure that the last two were not allowed to girls until they were
married. They liked Thackeray pretty well, Bulwer very well, and Dickens
they read under protest—they thought him low. They felt an easy sense of
superiority in being 'quite English in our tastes, you know,' and knew little
of the literature of their own country, as it came chiefly from the North. Of
its lesser lights they had never heard, and as for the greater, they would
have pitted an ounce of Poe against a pound of any one of them. The women
of Yariba read more than the men; the men were modelled after the heroes
that the women loved.[43]

Surely Sherwood's father's library greatly increased her interest in
literature and contributed enormously to her chosen profession.

The third most influential factor upon the young Sherwood Bonner was her formal education. None of the early biographers comment specifically upon her early schooling, other than to state that
she attended the public schools of Holly Springs; but it is known
that she was enrolled at the age of ten in the Holly Springs Female
Institute. Tuition statements from this school show that she was a
pupil of that institution from June 30, 1859, through the session
ending in February, 1862, when the normal routine of the schools at
Holly Springs was disrupted by the Civil War.[44] These receipted
tuition bills show that Sherwood was a regular student in the
Academic Department of the Institute in 1859 and 1860 and that she
was promoted to the Collegiate Department in 1861.[45]

Besides the regular academic subjects offered by these departments, she also undertook the study of French and Music.[46] Her
primary interest was apparently English and possibly English Composition, for one of the tuition bills shows an extra charge of one
dollar for "extra stationery for writing."[47] Furthermore, one of her
early biographers notes that, "although many girls in her classes
dreaded the weekly themes and compositions, Kate took real pleasure in them, and because of the papers she turned in . . . she was

the object of envy among her admiring friends who struggled with sentences and paragraphs."[48] It is a matter of record that Sherwood herself was to claim later, in the personage of Blythe Herndon, the heroine of *Like Unto Like*, to have "written the graduating compositions for half the girls in her class."[49] Still another biographer suggests that the youthful Bonner was precocious "in history, literature and composition, but rather backward in other branches. Said she, 'Life is too short for geometry.' "[50]

In addition to the rather meager information afforded by the surviving records of Sherwood Bonner's schooling, there are two descriptions of the young Bonner that present an unusually detailed characterization of Sherwood during her school days in Holly Springs. The first is, according to family sources, by a fellow classmate and was written when Sherwood was about twelve years old.[51] The sketch is entitled "Saint Katherine":

When you look at her face, in its aureole of guinea-golden hair, the first feature noticed was nose; a peculiar one; not large, yet very forcible, and indicative of ability to the advancement of its fair owner in any direction toward which her aspirations tended.

Next you would observe the mouth, being most like to find there either a kind, sweet smile or a bright playful half-laugh; but were these absent the sweet lips fell into a melancholy—sweeter if possible than either smile or laugh—this drooping expression by the way, I finally ascertained to be habitual when she was alone.

In looking for her eyes, one must first ever have remarked the forehead, with its slight retreat, and heavy base which overhung the eyes—eyes like the sky of a Northern sunrise, making the saddened soul of weakly ones to glow, even as the gray-blue light of morning freshens the erstwhile darkened earth. Such as her gaze of love, but when her righteous anger was aroused, those eyes would give one quick look—that one look all sufficient, and then deigning no more notice she would turn with a scornful lifting of her expressive lip and leave the object of her contempt in mingled wonder and humiliation. She never relied on words for the expression of her anger.

Her gentle bearing was stately as a queen's; but when joyed at the meeting of some dear friend or lover she would glide as swiftly to meet them, as I have seen an autumn tinted maple leaf wander gracefully in midair seemingly independent of common law until catching sight of the clear lake it would dart toward it with a quick flutter at thought of union with its love.

Her soul was all Truth, Honor, Charity, and filled with saint-like love; and the music of good deeds had made a full high harmony of her life but that the chord of hope was loosened and sent forth a melancholy sound, which though it sweetened that harmony made it the less cheering.[52]

The second description of the young Bonner is in Sherwood's own words; a characterization of the heroine of *Like Unto Like*, this sketch, according to one of Sherwood's great-nephews, is as accurate a picture of young Sherwood as could be conceived:

Perhaps if Blythe had been more popular among the young people she would have absorbed herself more happily in the usual interests of a girl in her father's home; but she had never been a favorite. She was called literary. This was an unfortunate adjective in Yariba, and set one rather apart from one's fellows, like an affliction in the family. Blythe's claims to the word, indeed, might not have been allowed in a Boston court, though she had read all the novels in Yariba, and thousands of old magazines. . . . On one occasion some callers were announced to her as she was reading an interesting book, and by the time it was finished she had forgotten their very existence. . . . Blythe had a power of sarcasm, too, that did not add to her popularity; and she was openly intolerant of mediocrity and narrowness, without suspecting her own arrogance.[53]

A consideration of young Catherine Sherwood during her first dozen years would be incomplete without a detailed presentation of the splendid mansion in which she spent a large portion of her brief life. The house was built by Dr. Charles Bonner when Catherine was nine years old, and she quickly accustomed herself to its library, the family parlor (where the formal entertaining took place), and Gran'mammy's domain, the separate kitchen. "Bonner House" as it was originally named, now called "Cedarhurst," still stands today, but the onetime lawn to the west of the house proper is now a paved thoroughfare appropriately called "Bonner Street." Despite the fact that the house now fronts on a United States highway, it is not difficult to imagine the house and the surrounding grounds as they existed during the lifetime of Sherwood Bonner. The following account of the Bonner house is from *Historic Homes of Mississippi:*

This home on Salem street, in the historic little city of Holly Springs, was built in 1858 by Dr. Charles Bonner, a native of Ireland. . . .

The home is a commodious brick mansion built in Gothic style, with windows opening to the floor, a wide portico in front, the roof supported by ten slender iron pillars, with handsome fret-work or iron joining the pillars. The balcony has the same design of fret-work in the balustrade that surrounds it. One enters a wide reception hall; on the left is the library peopled with books, bright with pictures, luxurious with soft-toned rugs and richly carved furniture; a big open wood fire-place, tiled in pale yellow, surmounted by a hardwood mantle, and with brass andirons, which were piled high with blazing logs whenever the frost-king overstepped the bounds of his domain. . . .

The library is connected with the hall by folding doors. On the right is the drawing room, also connected with the hall by folding doors. When these doors open, the whole front of the house is converted into one grand room. The family was preeminently literary, and the literateurs of the country often visited there; and then the grand drawing room was ablaze with light that 'shone o'er fair women and brave men,' it was a scene of delight.

There are four large bedrooms on the second floor, with double windows in front and long narrow ones on the sides. In the rear yard, and remote from the dwelling, as was the custom in days gone by, are the servants' quarters, the kitchen and store rooms. Beyond these lie the vegetable gardens and orchards, which were planted by Dr. Bonner.[54]

This magnificent mansion was not long to remain solely in the hands of the Bonner family, for war between the North and South was already threatening. The Civil War directly affected the life of Sherwood Bonner in many ways: it brought an end to her formal schooling; it presented her with a wealth of experiences that she later used; and it gave her the independence that characterized her adult life.

III   *The Trying Years: Groping for Stability*

Less than four years after the Bonners had moved into their ornate and beautifully furnished home, it was taken over by federal troops to quarter general officers. The Civil War years were of tremendous significance in shaping the developing career of Sherwood Bonner, for during this time she was at perhaps the most impressionable of years. Initially, young Sherwood herself, like the majority of the residents of Holly Springs, was caught in the excitement of an event that she herself was to call "but a promise of victory."[55] In 1876, at the age of twenty-seven, drawing from material she had recorded in her diaries and scrapbooks, Sherwood Bonner recalled vividly these wartime years in an autobiographical reminiscence entitled "From '60 to '65."[56] She remembers with enthusiasm how, at the age of twelve, she sealed her devotion to the Southern cause:

The first cannon made in the South was moulded at the Hollywell foundry. It was a great day when the work was begun. Crowds of people were outside the building, and as many as were allowed to enter were within.

Standing there amid the din and whir of machinery, while the sooty-faced
workmen hurried hither and thither, and the great furnace roared and
reddened, the hour was pregnant with grand significance. As the melted
ore poured forth a woman's hand held under it the great iron ladle and
emptied it into the mould with the solemnity of a priestess assisting at a holy
rite. Every woman and child followed in turn. It was our consecration to the
cause—an hour that I cannot remember now without a thrill of emotion akin
to that which thrilled me to the very centre of my being as I clasped my
hands around the iron handle and felt that in that moment I sealed my
devotion to the South.[57]

When war finally did come to Holly Springs, it arrived with terrible suddenness. In early December of the same year, 1862, word
came of the advance of the Union forces; and the "gray-coated
officers" of the balls, the reviews, and the gay dinners left Holly
Springs:

It was a sad day when the army left, for we bade friends good-bye to
prepare for foes. Boxes of silver were buried at night under flower-beds or
ash-heaps; gold-pieces were secured in leather belts; doors were locked and
windows barred. Then we waited until one bright morning in December,
when frightened negroes came flying in from the country round with the
dread news. 'The Yankees are coming!' They came, with the sound of music
and the beating of drums, into a silent town. From behind closed blinds we
listened to the tread of their advancing feet or peeped timidly at the blue
ranks, marching by. Before sundown the pleasant groves of Hollywell were
dotted with white tents, the stars and stripes fluttered from a high flag-pole,
and from the park the inspiring strains of 'Yankee Doodle' seemed to mock
our impotent anger and bitter humiliation.[58]

One event lessened the humiliation before the Southern cause
took on its hopeless air and before Holly Springs was to taste forever
the bitterness and deprivation that war has universally inflicted
upon all civilians. Although fate chose to shine upon the fortunes of
Holly Springs for but a single day, it was a day that left an inefface-
able impression on the youthful Sherwood Bonner. Shortly after
mid-December, 1862, General U.S. Grant, storing the bulk of his
supplies in the same foundry in which the first cannon made in the
South had been cast, passed through the city on his way to the
Mississippi Gulf Campaign; but he left behind him a skeleton guard
to protect "his ammunition and commissary supplies." Upon this
occasion, as Sherwood Bonner describes it,

Van Dorn seized the opportunity to make a raid into Hollywell. The day—
'The *Glorious*, GLORIOUS Twentieth,' I find it called in my diary of that
date—has become for ever memorable in the Hollywell annals. The confed-
erates dashed in early in the morning, surprising the sleeping camp and
gaining a surrender without a fight. The people were frantic with joy, ready
to make an idol of the general. . . . The air was alive with the shrill cry,
'Hurrah! hurrah for General Van Dorn!' A Federal colonel had chosen our
house as his headquarters, and Van Dorn paid him the compliment of a call.
He had a very handsome sword that had been presented to him by the
ladies of his native place, and he bit his lip angrily as he gave it up. Van
Dorn handed it back to him with a courteous bow, to the surprise and
gratification of the irate colonel, who from that moment accepted things
with a good grace. His wife, however, was furious enough for two; never
were frowns so black or tones so sharp; her pale anger as she snapped out
remarks about 'rebel devils' was a joy to my Southern soul. I innocently
inquired why her people had come South if they did not want to be so badly
treated.

'To make you *behave* yourselves; and we're going to *do* it, too,' said she
fiercely.

I waved my hand toward the road where a squad of blue coats was
passing, escorted by a rebel guard, and said in a melancholy voice, 'It looks
like it: it does, indeed!' This joke cost me dear, for two days later we were
turned out of our house through the colonel's representations, but nothing
could take away the satisfaction that had been mine for one perfect day.[59]

At the time of this particular incident, Catherine Sherwood was only
thirteen years old; and she still undoubtedly regarded the conflict as
something remote from her and from the life in Holly Springs, but
the next two years changed markedly both her concept of war and
her attitude toward "the Yankee invaders."

The forced removal of the Bonner family from its home following
the return of Grant's army was probably largely responsible for
Sherwood's attendance at a fashionable girl's school in Montgomery,
Alabama, from January through June of 1863. The school was called
either Hamner Hall or the Diocesan Female Seminary, and it was
affiliated with the Episcopal Church.[60] Sherwood's own account of
this brief period of her life is most cursory, but it indicates that the
realities of war, harsh and inevitable, were beginning to present
themselves to the young Bonner for thoughtful consideration.

The destruction of his stores forced Grant to bring back his soldiers. They
wreaked their vengeance on Hollywell as they passed through it a second

time, and then left it to its old quiet. For the next six months I was at
boarding school in Montgomery, Alabama. Here again I saw the bright side
of the war. To be sure, our preceptor had an unpleasant way of holding up a
slice of beef on the end of his fork and telling us how much it cost, and we
had to give sixty dollars a pair for very ill-fitting shoes; but these were minor
evils that we bore with the easy philosophy of youth. The city was delightfully gay; General Joe Johnston was there a part of the time with his staff,
and, school-girls though we were, we had more than an occasional glimpse
of our military heroes in concert or ball-room.[61]

If Sherwood had found only the price of meat and shoes outra-
geous in Montgomery, Alabama, she was to see and recognize fully
for perhaps the first time upon her return to Holly Springs in the
summer of 1863 the awful price that war inevitably exacts from even
the innocent. The brief buggy ride from the railroad station to
"Bonner House" was sufficient to reveal to Sherwood the toll taken
by the various raids upon Holly Springs and its surrounding countryside, raids by both North and South that were to number sixty
before Lee's surrender brought a semblance of peace and a partial
return to near-normalcy.[62] Again Catherine Sherwood's own description of the scene of desolation, coupled with her sense of horror
and outrage as she gazed upon objects and scenes she had come to
revere, is most suggestive of the deepening depression that the war
produced on Sherwood Boonner:

In the summer I went back to Hollywell, and not until then did I realize
the desolation that follows in the track of war. The town was cut off from
communication with the outside world, except for a handcar that ran between the towns on the Mississippi road. . . . In the afternoon of a long hot
day I stepped off the car at the village station. . . . I should never have
recognized in that dreary village the once prosperous, comfortable, little
town. Rank weeds grew everywhere, and desolation hung over all things
like a funeral pall. Where the town-hall had stood was now a shapeless heap
of brick and mortar overgrown with nettles and dog-fennel. The door of the
old church where we had worshipped from one generation to another had
been torn away, and, looking in, I saw the organ bereft of its pipes, the
pulpit of its cushions. The seats were broken up, and not a pane of glass was
left in the windows. Even in the graveyard the destroyer had been at work:
the gravestones were toppled over, and upon the white columns yet standing were scrawled rude jests and caricatures. The flowers were dry and
dead: a few melancholy cows were cropping the weeds that had overgrown
the once-sacred graves. Here and there a mouldy coffin-lid was thrown out

upon the upturned sod. The schoolhouse was leveled to the ground, but its red chimneys stood, like faithful sentinels, over the ruined pile. Private dwellings, too, were gone, and in their stead were hastily-erected cabins through whose open doors we caught glimpses of black-robed figures. The square was deserted, except by a company of small boys, who were marching round it in soldier-fashion, and a few old men with long white hair, who were dozing in the sun.[63]

The people of Holly Springs had also changed with the changing fortunes of the South's cause, and one of the first persons that Sherwood encountered on that memory-stricken day of her return was a woman, perched comfortably on top of three bales of cotton riding in an ox-wagon, whom she failed to recognize. When informed that the woman was Mrs. Herrick, Sherwood "gave such a start that the crazy buggy almost tipped over," for this woman had been the wife of "one of the richest planters in our state, noted for her pride and aristocratic prejudices."[64] She was then told by one of her cousins that Mrs. Herrick was now considered "one of our best blockade-runners. . . . The Yanks have the women searched now as they pass the picket-lines, but they can't get ahead of a first-class smuggler like Mrs. Herrick."[65]

The six-month period during which Sherwood Bonner had been in Montgomery attending fashionable Hamner Hall had indeed changed Holly Springs forever. Sherwood's younger sister, Ruth, later recounted to her grandchildren her recollections of standing on the front porch of "Bonner House" watching while many of the country homes were burned by the Yankee soldiers, and as many as thirteen were set afire in a single night.[66] The town homes were generally spared, "largely because they were used to quarter troops and as headquarters for the officers."[67] This practice of the Union forces probably led Catherine Sherwood's aunt, Mrs. Ellen Hopeton, who "lived alone on a small plantation three miles from Hollywell," to take Sherwood to live with her for the next several months. Aunt Ellen was a practical Southerner, who, according to Sherwood, "tried to play the part of England in the fight and keep in with both sides. To the Yankees she would talk of 'my nephew, Charles Hopeton, in Sherman's army,' with more than a maternal fondness, when the fact was that this youth was a degenerate and far-off relative whose face she had never seen."[68] Sherwood adds that Aunt Ellen was on safer grounds with the rebels, "for 'my son, Colonel Albert Hopeton,' was well known throughout the country, and his mother's loyalty was never doubted in spite of her politeness to the enemy."[69] Most of the Aunt Ellens of the South did not believe that this duplicity in any way betrayed their cause; they felt, as Sherwood Bonner points out, that such tactics were necessary in order to protect their homes, land, and possessions for the eventual return of the husbands, fathers, sons, and brothers who were fighting for the cause in which all so completely believed.[70]

Despite the hardships of the times, ones frequently compounded by the presence of the Union forces, the people of Holly Springs got along well with the occupation armies; and, it must be admitted, the young ladies of Holly Springs attended with almost equal enthusiasm the gay military balls given in honor of both the Northern and Southern forces.[71] For most of the time during the Northern army occupation of Holly Springs, "Bonner House" was used as the headquarters for General Ord of General Grant's staff; and a warm and respectful friendship developed between Dr. Charles Bonner and the Yankee general.[72] Such was not the case, initially at least, with the younger and more spirited Sherwood.

It is a well-known tale among descendants of the Bonner family that none of the Bonner's three children would pass under the American flag which hung over the front porch of "Bonner House" whenever the house was occupied by a federal officer. In her autobiographical novel, *Like Unto Like*, Sherwood Bonner recalls this specific incident when, commenting in the person of Blythe Herndon upon the attitude of Southern women during the Civil War, she remarks that "the Northern troops were in Yariba half the time during the war, and we women of Yariba were not behind others in showing loyalty to our cause. When this house was taken for a hospital, and the Union flag hung over the porch, rather than walk under it, I went out through the windows or jumped off the end of the porch."[73]

This attitude of defiance did not remain long with Sherwood, however, and there is evidence of a softening in it even as early as mid-1863, during the six months that she was living with her aunt, Mrs. Hopeton. She "confesses" in a diary entry of 1863 that she had written that a Yankee soldier may even be a gentleman, and finally in the same entry she goes so far as to state that "I have come to the conclusion that a man may be in the Northern army and yet be an honest man."[74] Several incidents narrated in her autobiographical writings on the Civil War years indicate her growing sympathy for both sides, and at one point she states categorically that "it is pleasant to remember that we often met with the utmost kindness from officers and men."[75] During one such meeting a band of drunk, noisy, and quarrelsome Yankee soldiers who had broken into the Hopeton stables were in the process of leading the mules away when Sherwood herself confronted the group to show them an order written by General Smith, U.S.A., authorizing Mrs. Hopeton to be "allowed to keep two mules." Sherwood unthinkingly surrendered the paper to one of the men to prove its authenticity, and her action was immediately greeted with a roar of laughter as one of the men said

'Well, you are a green 'un! Don't you know that he can tear up that paper, and do what he likes with the mules and you too?'

I was frightened enough, but my mother wit came to my aid, and I said with a smile worthy of Aunt Ellen herself, 'I trust his honor as a gentleman.'

It may have been his intention to destroy it, but he handed it back with a shamefaced expression, and said, 'Well, miss, you've got plenty of pluck, so you hev. If you'll just shake hands all round we'll leave you the mules. What d'ye say, boys?'

There was a shout of approval. I very willingly submitted to the rough hand-shaking, and went back to Aunt Ellen with triumph.[76]

In the fall of the same year, 1863, an incident occurred that for some reason is not alluded to at all by Sherwood Bonner, either in her fiction or autobiographical reminiscences; but the event surely must have affected the young girl. On November 29, 1863, Catherine Sherwood's youngest sister, Anne Lea Bonner, then but four years old, died.[77] Sherwood's niece, Mrs. Ruth McDowell Stephenson, a Bonner family historian who based her information on private family papers, attributed the death of Anne Lea to excitement and exposure accompanying the forced removal of the Bonner family from its home by the invading Yankees.[78] The attribution is probably an exaggerated one, but the Bonners were forcibly evicted on several occasions from "Bonner House" in order to allow high-ranking Yankee officers to set up their headquarters there, and one such incident did occur in late 1863, when General McPherson was temporarily installed in the mansion.[79]

The situation in Holly Springs during the winter of 1863–1864 must have been extremely depressing for a fourteen-year-old girl to contemplate. Many of Sherwood Bonner's stories with a Civil War setting reveal quite plainly the poverty and deprivation endured by the Bonner family in the last years of the conflict. Frequent references appear, for example, to a lack of bedding, a scarcity of meat, and total lack of decent coffee beans. Sherwood shows in many of her stories that, for the greater part of the war years, the people of Holly Springs actually drank coffee made from goober peas and sweet potatoes.[80]

Even the bitterest of the war years, however, were not without their moments of thanksgiving. The third story in the "Gran'mammy" section of the *Suwanee River Tales* collection, entitled "How Gran'mammy Broke the News," is a true account of how the Bonner family reacted to the news of the death of one of the family favorites. Allan Edmandson, the kin reported killed in battle, was the youngest son of Sherwood's Aunt Sarah Edmandson, who was at that time living with the Bonner family in Holly Springs because her own neighboring plantation home had been destroyed by a roving party of Yankee raiders in the first year of the war. The events depicted in this story may suggest the beginning of Sherwood's attitude of reconciliation in regard to the North versus South conflict. As is true with most of the Civil-War-setting stories, Sherwood plays herself, appearing throughout the story as "young Kate." The point of the story is not the death of Allan, but his unexpected appearance at "Bonner House" after he had been reported as killed on the battlefield. His recovery had been effected through the tender regard and medical skill of a Yankee soldier who found young Allan dying and abandoned by his own forces as either already dead or mortally wounded. Nursed back to health by the Union soldier, he was then released in a prisoner exchange to rejoin his family in the South. Young Sherwood's feelings of gratitude for the unknown Yankee soldier who had rescued and saved her favorite cousin develop into the sympathetic understanding and spirit of forgiveness that become the principal theme of her only novel, *Like Unto Like*. As Sherwood expressed it in the "Gran'mammy" story,

Happy and thankful were those Southern hearts that blessed Christmas eve; and the prayer breathed so fervently from us all may, I hope, by chance meet the eye of him for whom it was made,—whose face we have never seen, whose name we have never known, but whose memory shall live with us forever.

God bless the Northern soldier! God reward him for the precious life he saved! And God grant, that some day, the Northern soldier and the Southern may meet, clasping hands as brave men and brothers,— if not on earth, in a fairer land, where the mists are cleared away, and we know, even as we are known.[81]

After the return of Allan Edmandson, the war lasted another seventeen months before the literal surrender of Lee made final the psychological one that had already taken place in the hearts of many loyal Southerners. These last several months differed only slightly, if at all, from the six months preceding the Christmas of 1863. In her autobiographical summary of the war years, Sherwood Bonner painfully recalls the passage of time that seemed an endless time of desolation: "The long summer wore away. The army went, winter came, and except for an occasional raid Hollywell was left in peace."[82] It was now the spring of 1865; and, despite the relative peace of their town, the people of Holly Springs still had daily reminders of the war and remained directly involved in it. The absence of the young men, many of whom were never to return; the sacrifices and deprivations of those left at home; and the occasional but ominous reports of battles fought and men killed kept the war continually in the minds of every citizen. Consequently, even the already defeated people of Holly Springs were not prepared for the capitulation of the South and its cause.[83] As Sherwood was to write of these last months, "We had no premonition that the end was near. . . . When the shock came it found us all unprepared. One spring day—the tenth of April, 1865—two ladies of Hollywell were busy collecting silver plate to be sent to Richmond and melted for the depleted treasury. They had just left our house, and I stood with them on the brow of a hill beyond."[84]

Despite the depressing news that came from the front lines, these women still remained utterly devoted to the Southern cause; and few at that time in Holly Springs, cut off from vital contact with the rest of the South, realized that all their sacrifices had been in vain—that, except for the formality of surrender, their cause was lost. The three women stood talking of the changes that had been wrought during the last several years—Sherwood, the youngest of the trio, now a young woman of sixteen; the war widow only one year her senior; and the older woman, also a victim of the war. In this setting, Sherwood Bonner heard the tragic news of Lee's surrender:

As we lingered for a few last words we saw Dr. Poindexter coming up the hill. He was a man of seventy, usually slow and stiff in his movements. Now his steps were rapid, almost a run. His long white hair floated out behind him, and once, twice, he threw his clasped hands above his head with a gesture of despair. We knew that he had a son in the army, and thought at once of some disaster to him.

'Jack is killed!' cried the young widow with a burst of tears.

We drew nearer together in trembling sympathy and waited for the grief-stricken father to pass. In the wild white face that he turned toward us there was such an agony as I have seen save in the face of a soldier in the hospital who had died an unlooked-for and horrible death. He looked at us a moment in silence, then in a hollow, harsh voice *struck* us with the words, 'General Lee has surrendered!' and passed on into the falling darkness.[85]

The sense of loss brought forth by the news of General Lee's surrender is best expressed by the final paragraph of Sherwood Bonner's wartime reminiscences: "Of the suffering of that after-time I have even now no words to speak. Its very memory is so terrible that I do not know how we endured it then. You, who have lost much, suffered much, for a cause that you have gained, cannot measure the sufferings of those who gave their all and lost."[86]

The news of the defeat of the South was not, however, the only depressing event of the year. Less than six months after Lee's surrender, Sherwood Bonner's mother, Mary Wilson Bonner, died at the age of thirty-seven on October 3, 1865. As has been noted, the descendants of the Bonner family felt that Mrs. Charles Bonner died of a broken heart, brought about by the suffering and poverty-stricken state of the Bonner family at the war's conclusion.[87] Sherwood Bonner's own description of her mother's death suggests the origin of such a belief: "And when the gentle mother whose life had been set to such sweet music that her spirit broke in the discords of dreadful war, sank out of life, it was in gran'mammy's arms that she died; and neither husband nor children mourned more tenderly for the beautiful life cut short."[88]

At the time of his wife's death, Dr. Charles Bonner was himself fifty-one years old, and there were still three young children in the Bonner family to be looked after: Catherine Sherwood, then sixteen; Ruth Bonner, only two years younger; and the only surviving son, Samuel Wilson Bonner, eleven years old. Whether Dr. Bonner had no intention of remarrying, or whether he simply felt that the children needed someone immediately to care for them, he sent at once for his sister, Martha Bonner, who was at that time teaching school in Penn Yan, New York.[89] "Auntee," as she was called by the Bonner children, arrived that same month; and she remained in Holly Springs for the rest of her life, caring first for the Bonner children, and later for Sherwood Bonner's own daughter, Lilian.

As black as were the Civil War years to Catherine Sherwood, especially the last two, they also brought to Sherwood her first short story publication, an event that had a lasting influence on her life. Her story, "Laura Capello, A Leaf from A Traveler's Notebook," had been sent when she was but fifteen years of age to Nahum Capen, the editor of the Boston *Ploughman*.[90] The young writer received twenty dollars for its publication, and her correspondence with Capen initiated the beginning of a long and important association for Sherwood.

During these last war years, the young girl also began reading serious literature, an interest that also had an important bearing on her own literary career. In the story "Coming Home to Roost" of the Suwanee River collection, Sherwood Bonner compares the death visions of the story's protagonist, Aunt Becky, to those of Ariel; and she confesses that she had "just begun to read Shakespeare."[91] Since Sherwood was sixteen years of age at the time at which the story occurs, one may assume that she was only now moving away from the juvenile books and tales that had occupied her attention during her earliest years. In this same year, the last of the Civil War years, Sherwood in one of her wartime reminiscences recalls going forth to do verbal battle with a marauding band of Yankee soldiers with a copy of H. W. Longfellow's *Hyperion* tucked under her arm.[92] In addition to her reading of Shakespeare and Keats during her sixteenth year, she also read frequently from her Bible; for, during the several months of her residence with her Aunt Ellen Hopeton, she was often called upon by her aunt to read to visiting Yankee soldiers from that most universal of all books:

Aunt Ellen, trusting in her peace policy, proposed that I should read the Bible aloud. 'I am sure these gentlemen would like to hear you,' she said with her pathetic smile: 'it will remind them of home.'

At the least show of anger or fear the men would have broken all bounds. I did not dare to refuse, but quietly opened my Bible.[93]

The years following the end of the Civil War were apparently just as quiet for Sherwood as was her reading from her Bible on that spring day of 1865. Undoubtedly they were years of prime impor-

tance to her, days of storing up additional memories of her
gran'mammy's stories, of life in Holly Springs, of impressions of
people she knew, and of other recollections that formed a large
reservoir of material from which she later drew for her early local-
color stories. And yet almost nothing is known of these formative
years. Since none of her early biographers makes any suggestion to
the contrary, and since it is an historical fact that the years following
the war were rather grim ones for much of the South, one may
reasonably assume that Sherwood remained for the most part in
Holly Springs, cultivated her always avid interest in literature, and
recorded in her diaries and journals incidents and characters that
were later described in her fiction.

Of the more pleasant side of life in Holly Springs during the
Reconstruction Era, historical records reveal that three companies
of federal troops were quartered in Holly Springs until 1866, and a
permanent garrison of 162 officers and men remained in the town
until 1875.[94] The presence of these soldiers in Holly Springs during
these years resulted in much more lively entertainment in the town
than would otherwise have been possible; and in her autobiographical novel, *Like Unto Like*, Sherwood details many of the friendships
that blossomed between Southern belles and Northern soldiers and
that were usually begun at one of the fancy military dress balls.
Apart from the autobiographical fiction, however, there exists one
other document to suggest life in Holly Springs during the days
of Reconstruction. If the only surviving diary in Sherwood Bonner's
hand, the diary for the year 1869, is at all representative of the postwar
years, and there is no reason to suspect that it is not, then a
fairly accurate picture of these years may be drawn from a careful
reading of the diary.

It opens with the announcement of preparations under way for a
visit to Mobile, Alabama, by way of New Orleans, Louisiana; and
Sherwood's last Sunday at home prior to her departure is spent
undertaking "a half arrangement of my valuable papers!" The entry
suggests an allusion to her diaries and journals, which she kept
rather consistently through at least her twentieth year. Undoubtedly these papers included a draft, if not a finished copy, of a short
story that she had been writing; for on January 21 she records mail-
ing a story identified only as her "Italian Story" to Nahum Capen,
then associated with the Boston *Sunday Times*. Apparently Sherwood had attempted few publications during the four years that

intervened between the acceptance of "Laura Capello" in 1865 and 1869. A search of nineteenth-century periodicals in which she published extensively has failed to turn up any other Bonner story prior to 1873.

However, two other items are referred to by Sherwood Bonner's earliest biographer, Professor Alexander Bondurant, who merely, notes that " 'Laura Capello' was followed by 'A Flower of the South,' published in a musical journal. Somewhat later a piece called 'An Exposition on one of the Commandments' was sent to *Frank Leslie's Journal*."[95] Since Professor Bondurant was engaged to Sherwood Bonner's daughter at the time of the publication of his biography of Sherwood Bonner,[96] he probably had access to private papers or diaries that have since disappeared. Even Bondurant, however, was unable to date the publication of either item; and his wording in connection with "An Exposition" implies that he is not certain that it was actually published. All subsequent biographers have included the two articles in their bibliographies of Bonner's work, but none has been able to locate either publication.

Sherwood Bonner did not have long to wait to hear from editor Capen regarding the submission of her "Italian Story," but she spent much of the next month "writing, reading, and talking."[97] Less than four weeks after the posting of the story in Mobile, Sherwood received a letter of acceptance from Capen and a check for twenty dollars, the identical sum which she had received for her first effort. Her interest in writing continued unabated, and less than three months after the acceptance of the "Italian Story" she recorded in her diary for May 12 that she had "Mailed exciting story without a name—all about a modern Quixote called Henry White." On this occasion, only ten days elapsed before she was again able to record "Letter from Mr. Capen—'Marion's Mistake' promptly accepted—Jubilate!"[98]

Although six years elapsed before Sherwood Bonner published another story, her literary interests during these years never waned; for her 1869 diary records numerous instances of her continued passion for reading. Although she makes no systematic attempt to include by title all, or even most, of the books that she read during this one year, she does mention specifically *Waverley* by Sir Walter Scott, *Villette* by Charlotte Bronte, *Griffith Gaunt* by Charles Reade, *Breaking a Butterfly* by George A. Lawrence, *The Count of Monte Cristo* by Alexandre Dumas, and the *Poems* of Percy Shelley,

the last a Christmas gift. Additionally, she mentions reading Alger-
non Swinburne aloud on three separate occasions with several of her
beaus and girlfriends and discussing not only Swinburne but also
Edgar Allan Poe, John Keats, and James Yates.[99]

Finally, in the same year, numerous entries reveal her constant
desire to enlarge upon her knowledge through a planned reading
program, such as when she proposes to read Immanuel Kant in
order to prepare for a forthcoming visit of a friend deeply interested
in philosophy, or when she simply records that she had recently
devoted much of her time to the reading of "a great many novels."
Not only were these books available in her father's library, but they
were also obtainable directly from the publishers, as indicated by
the announcements and advertisements carried in the local papers;
in addition, Holly Springs possessed a bookstore, for on two occasions during 1869 Sherwood records meeting friends there. As
further evidence of her deep passion for reading, there is the statement in *Like Unto Like* that she "had read all the novels in Yariba,
and thousands of old magazines."[100]

Besides documenting her literary interests, the diary for 1869 also
reveals another fascinating aspect of Sherwood's personality and
temperament—a recurring depression that at times borders on the
hysterical. As early as January 7, she records feeling "depressed in
spirit because of my strange lack of interest in all things of earth—
No regret at leaving home—no joy in thinking of pleasure to
come—I can not build a castle in the air." A little over a month later,
on the occasion of her twentieth birthday, Friday, February 26, she
returns to this melancholy theme: "My birthday! having known
some nineteen others, such things have become common, & I can't
say that I very heartily echo the kind wishes for 'Many Returns' of
the same. Twenty years! 'nor peace within nor calm around!' To
express myself I should sketch a rudderless ship upon a stormy
ocean." Only three days later she was to add that "every day I live I
become more & more hopeless of happiness—more disgusted with
myself & all mankind."[101]

One can only speculate about the reason or reasons for these
periods of depression, but a careful consideration of the hints expressed throughout the diary reveals that a rational explanation of
such moods need not be wholly without foundation. A young, proud
girl, already twenty, was engaged to a man with whom she was not
in love, and she was also rebelling against the narrow confines of a

small-town society that she openly resented. A girl more gifted than most others, she saw the possibility of escaping from the conventions of Southern society lessen with each succeeding day.

Sherwood Bonner later expressed her longing for a different life in her autobiographical novel and recalled her determination to escape from the small Southern community in which she had been reared: "I cannot tell you how I long for life, movement, action. I am so tired of this place!—the quiet streets, the hills and the streams, and the moss eternally waving. I want to get away from it all. Nothing ever happens here. And only think—there are people living here who are old, and who have never been out of Yariba! Fancy having written against one's name in the book of fate only this:—was born,—married,—died."[102] As the year wears on, it becomes increasingly evident to the careful reader of the diary that more was to be written after the name of Catherine Sherwood Bonner; for on September 4 she recorded the conviction that "marriage is not to sink *me* into a drudge of nonentity, whatever it may do for weaker sisters."

That the tantalizing prospects of a literary career continued to create a barrier between Sherwood and any reasonable hope for a satisfactory marriage is suggested by an entry for September 13 in which she announces her intention "to go through a course of study this winter, renounce society, & devote myself to French, German and music." In the same month, three weeks later, she reiterated this pledge: "I intend to give up society this winter & devote myself to writing and studying. Every one tells me I could make of myself what I would & I am determined to make one last effort."[103] Might it not reasonably be conjectured that Sherwood intended that nothing should finally prevent her pursuit of a literary career, not even her forthcoming marriage to Edward McDowell, and could not this conflict itself be largely responsible for her recurring moods of depression? Future events suggest such was indeed the case.

Although many entries in the 1869 diary imply that Sherwood was not convinced of her love for Edward McDowell, even more significantly two entries actually foreshadow her separation from Edward after a little less than two years of marriage and their subsequent divorce. In a comment that implies a possible application to a great many areas, and especially to relationships with other people, Sherwood had written on January 2 that "nothing in life has power to make me miserable save a wound given to pride. This can only make my heart sick with despair." Catherine Sherwood Bonner was a proud girl and an even prouder woman. She never accepted defeat or resigned herself to an untenable position. Ten months later, in commenting on the terribly deprived life that unfortunate economic circumstances had forced upon one of her schoolmates, Sherwood wrote: "Poor Laura! I fear she is not happy tho' she is devoted to Mr. Robinson. But such a life as she leads would I should think be enough to make any woman miserable—Buried in the country, in bad health, no cook half the time, without a nurse all the time, with nothing but drudgery & slavery before her—I can't see how she endures it— If I thought this was to be my fate I would kill myself now—"[104] These various comments, coupled with the recurring appeal of a literary career, help to create an understanding of the personality and temperament of Sherwood Bonner at the end of these, her most formative years.

The only other relevant information that the diary of 1869 contains suggests the principal events of the Reconstruction years. There are parties, picnics, and, for the most part, regular Sunday church attendance. There are occasional weekends spent with country relatives and infrequent trips to New Orleans, Memphis, and Mobile. There are incessant dances and socials, attended by college youths from the nearby University of Mississippi as well as by the officers and men of the federal garrison. Despite the misgivings about her forthcoming marriage, and despite occasional emotional outbursts caused by the lack of interesting activities in Holly Springs, the postwar years served as a significant preparation for the literary life that Sherwood Bonner was soon to lead; and they were not totally dismal times, as she confided in one of the last entries for the year: "On the whole I find myself tolerably happy this Christmas time—altogether happier than I have been for years."[105] Regrettably, this happiness did not endure beyond her twenty-first year.

Since Sherwood Bonner began her serious writing career almost immediately after her marriage to Edward McDowell and after the end of the Civil War, the question as to what part the war itself played in her resolve to enter the writing profession deserves brief consideration. There is no doubt, of course, that the war, the occupation by Northern armies, and the Reconstruction Era provided Sherwood Bonner with a wealth of information and material that would much later find its way into her fiction. But, if one considers carefully Sherwood's early and sustained interest in writing and books—beginning with her first efforts at creative writing in the Holly Springs Female Seminary and enduring through numerous entries in her diary for 1869—one comes to the inevitable conclusion that she would have attempted a literary career even had there been no Civil War. That the war helped her to mature more rapidly—to become at an early age self-reliant and independent—may be true. The war and the effects of the war on the Bonner family and on Holly Springs itself may well have confirmed Sherwood in her desire to write movingly and tellingly of wartime conditions. But, to this observer at least, Sherwood felt called upon to write; and the war and its consequences merely provided more material to draw upon in her later fiction.

CHAPTER 2

The Productive Years

I Getting Started: Marriage, Separation, and Boston

A little over a year after the last entry in her 1869 diary was
written, Sherwood Bonner, the numerous misgivings over her
approaching marriage temporarily forgotten or resolved, fulfilled
her intention of marrying Edward McDowell. Appropriately, or
perhaps ironically in view of the subsequent divorce, the young
couple chose Valentine's Day for the date of the wedding ceremony;
and on February 14, 1871, Edward McDowell, late of Louisiana,
and Catherine Sherwood Bonner of Holly Springs were married at
the Christ Episcopal Church in Holly Springs.[1]

Admittedly, some contradictory statements concerning Edward
McDowell exist, but they are not overly important in their particulars. Most early biographers of Sherwood Bonner agree that "Mr.
Edward McDowell, a gentleman of refinement and liberal culture,"
was, like his wife, "a native of Holly Springs."[2] Yet the official entry
in the parish record clearly shows him to be from Louisiana. His
immediate background is also obscured by testimony he gave at the
custody trial over Lilian McDowell when he stated that he had been
educated in England.[3] Since, however, Sherwood Bonner's diary
for 1869 details several meetings that took place in Holly Springs
during that year and since Sherwood's sister Ruth later married
Edward's brother David, there seems little reason to question seri-
ously the impression that both parties were residents of Holly
Springs at the time of their marriage. The confusion is cleared partly
by Dorothy Gilligan's statement that the family of Edward
McDowell, like the family of Dr. Charles Bonner, came originally
from Ireland. It is, therefore, certainly possible that Edward could
have been educated abroad, reared in Holly Springs, and maintained at the time of the marriage his actual legal residence in
Louisiana.

There is not a great deal known about the early months of the young couple's marriage. All previous biographical accounts dispose of the marriage in two or three paragraphs and move directly from Holly Springs in 1870 to Boston in 1873 in tracing Sherwood Bonner's life. Such treatment is largely justified, for the marriage probably deserves no more than passing mention. From hints in the later letters of Sherwood Bonner and from testimony given during her divorce suit and the later custody trial for Lilian, it may be stated without fear of contradiction that Edward was primarily an irrepressible and irresponsible dreamer. In the space of a few years' time, he went from one grandiose scheme for making a quick fortune to another, from investing heavily in gold mines in Georgia to pursuing a method for gathering bat-cave guano along the Louisiana and Texas Gulf Coast. Apparently, Sherwood and Edward made their home in Holly Springs for approximately a year and a half after their marriage, but Edward ventured forth occasionally into neighboring states to investigate various promising schemes.[4] An excerpt from a family paper is relevant in this connection:

Mr. Edward McDowell . . . was of fine family and brilliant education but was always an impractical dreamer, a visionary with wild schemes for making money in Texas and other frontier regions. A daughter was born to the young couple, and when she, Lilian, was little more than a year old, Mr. and Mrs. McDowell set out for the Lone Star State to make a fortune in a project that was surpassed in wildness only by the later bat-cave guano scheme by which Mr. McDowell was confident he would make 'at least a million dollars.' This scheme, like all others he attempted, was doomed to failure by its very impracticability. Kate wrote back home 'My heart fairly aches to see you all.' In these long days in Texas she remembered the few stories she had sold, and realizing that her husband could never succeed in any of his ventures, she decided to go to Boston to make a literary name for herself.[5]

Edward McDowell's testimony in the custody trial for Lilian, the only other source that comments at all on the early years of the Bonner-McDowell marriage, adds little to this account. He merely alludes to the couple's separation when he implies that it was Sherwood who abandoned him, despite the fact that he was earning a satisfactory living for his family: "I was in business in my own right in Dallas, Texas. Lilian and her mother were with me about four months. My wife & child left Dallas in 1873. I sent them to my

mother's till September of that year."[6] Edward apparently expected
Sherwood and Lilian to await his return to Holly Springs after he
had finished his Dallas venture, but he seems not to have been
surprised by Sherwood's almost immediate departure for Boston.
According to the custody trial testimony, Edward made no attempt
to undertake the care of his family during any part of the next and
the last ten years of the life of Catherine Sherwood Bonner.
Whether Sherwood's actions in leaving her husband without confid-
ing her plans to him were justified or not, the fact remains that she
did leave. In the words of Miss Sophia Kirk, Bonner's closest companion during her last several months, "pecuniary troubles led her
to take up the pen as a means of support" although Sherwood "had
barely passed the borders of girlhood, though already a wife and
mother."[7]

The exact date of Sherwood Bonner's departure from Holly
Springs for Boston is unknown, but it may be approximately ascertained. She wrote to her family from Uvalde, Texas, on July 18,
1873, complaining of her wretched state; and, on October 12 of that
same year, Dr. Charles Bonner received the following letter from
Nahum Capen.[8] Apparently Sherwood Bonner had lost no time
after arriving in Boston in looking up the only contact she had with
literary Boston, a contact which paved the way toward the limited
success that she enjoyed as a local-color writer during the next ten
and a half years:

Boston, Oct. 12th, '73

My dear Sir,
    Altho' a stranger to you personally,—I feel that we are together in feeling
and sentiment,—and by the partiality of your daughter—under the same
bond of sympathy and duty—
    By seeing letters of mine to another—giving encouragement to a young
and wounded spirit,—your daughter Katherine [sic] imagined that she
could derive benefit from my counsel. . . .
    It is but proper that I should say, however—that I enjoined upon her the
sacred duty of consulting her father in all things; and to trust him above all
other men—in respect to the means of success and happiness. After she was
married—I again turned her to her father and to her husband for
counsel—not being willing to advise her on any question until they had
spoken. After her arrival in Boston she told me that you were ignorant of
her plans and purposes. She did not pursue this course she says because she
did not respect and honor you—but because she felt that she was not equal
to giving sufficient reasons to satisfy your judgment that she was right.

Her aspirations were stronger than her sense of duty, that is, she felt that she must first do justice to herself, to her own powers, before she could do justice to others. She has imposed upon herself a course of severe labor—and a condition of deprivation to accomplish her ends.

It seemed to be a remarkable case of self-imposed duty and discipline. From the first I have counseled her in a way that all good fathers could approve in fact. I have done what I feel would be right and kind in another extended to my own children.

Your daughter has a very active mind,—more ideas and fancies than her judgment has been able to control. She is doubtless a mystery to herself. She has high aspirations—and she has been unhappy because she could not find or see the means for their development and realization.

We have one of the best schools for the education of Young Ladies—in the world—and it is free to all our citizens. I have as a citizen procured her admission into this school—and she is pursuing her studies with great zeal and cheerfulness. She boards near the school—and at very small expense. Her hours of study and studies pursued—she will tell you herself.

A self-imposed discipline—made to gratify peculiar tastes or wants—is the severest when adopted in good faith—and it is to be hoped that the chosen path of your daughter will prove a blessing not only to herself—but to all who are entitled to her love. I write by her request—and be assured, My dear Sir, that there are no privileges in this world so precious to a good heart—as the privilege of doing good to others. . . . Believe me ever, Sir,

Ever and faithfully your friend,

Nahum Capen[9]

Dr. Chas. Bonner
Holly Springs,
Miss.

At the time of the arrival of Sherwood Bonner in Boston, Nahum Capen was sixty-nine years old, and both the tone and commentary of his letter to Dr. Bonner suggest that Capen quickly began to think of the young Sherwood as one of his own daughters. Sophia Kirk has noted that Capen initially employed Sherwood as his personal secretary and that she fulfilled a role somewhat similar to the one which she later undertook for Longfellow.[10] Dorothy Gilligan states that Sherwood helped Capen in the drafting and revising of his well-received *History of Democracy*, a not improbable assignment since Capen recommended Bonner to Longfellow as his amanuensis in the compilation of *Poems of Places*. Moreover, Capen would not have been willing to recommend an assistant to Longfellow unless he himself had some personal knowledge of her abilities in such a capacity.

These first few months in 1873 in Boston, despite the encouragement given Sherwood by Capen, were difficult and often hungry times; for Sherwood still possessed more than a normal allotment of pride. A letter to her sister, Ruth Bonner, written the following month, comments on both the financial difficulties she labored under and the status of her marriage:

Boston, Mass.
Nov. 13th, 1873

My dear Ruthie

Your letter just this moment received has almost put me beside myself with my longing for my baby. I don't know how I can live without her through this dreary winter, but I do feel that it will be for the best good of all concerned for me to stay. It is imperative that I learn how to work and to deny myself—and heaven knows I am doing it now.

I have faith that I will succeed in my writings. The more I see of other minds and the more I understand the literature of the day, the more certain I am of my own capability to take a rank not very high perhaps, but high enough to earn my own bread and butter at least; which will be that much saved for poor Edward. I have vowed never to cost him another cent, and perhaps if those who blame me in my present course *knew all which no one that lives will ever* they would judge me far differently—As for writing to Edward I have done so again and again, and in confidence I tell you that since coming to Boston I have received *just one letter*, which was written he said simply to inform me that we were beggars—and that he took no interest in my present course—that after solemnly vowing that I might go to T. [could she have meant B. for Boston?] and in every way assuring me of his cooperation in my plans before I left Texas—and I now find that he was only making a fool of me as he has done from first to last; deceiving me by a pretended consent so that he could induce me to leave him and go home where he thought you would all prevent me from carrying out my plans! . . .

After several paragraphs of comments about the encouragement and generosity of Nahum Capen, Sherwood's letter concludes with a brief resume of her daily routine:

I commenced taking my meals two a day at a house next door to my lodging place that advertised for table boarders. Dinner and supper every day, $2.50 per week. I stood it for three meals, food very good, but table manners of daughters too much for my appetite, notwithstanding my own terrible failing in table etiquette. So I cracker and cheese it in my room as it is too cold to go to a restaurant. I don't know what would become of me but for ginger snaps. They are to me as brother, sister, friend. They cost less and go further and taste better than any other two things you can mention. It is most remarkable that I never taste meat—I have to trot up and down with coal and things. . . . I have had to stop my music owing to no money. . . .[11]

Despite the lack of money and the sacrifices she was obliged to make—undoubtedly her pride and the implication of an early defeat prevented her from writing home for funds—Sherwood immediately attempted to get some of her earlier stories accepted by periodical editors. Initially, she met rejection on every side; but the critical comments accompanying some of the letters of rejection proved invaluable to her. Theodore W. Dwight, a New York critic who made no promise to reexamine the stories submitted, or others, at a later date, was of enormous help in pinpointing one of the chief defects of Bonner's early work:

If you had considered it of sufficient importance to rewrite parts of them, I would have been glad to submit them to my good friend, the Editor of the *Overland Monthly.* I think you have real power for story writing, your fancy is very exuberant, and if you would pay close attention to detail, the construction of sentences and choice of words, I do not think you would find any difficulty in developing your plot or realizing your characters naturally and artistically. The only considerable fault I found was, that the influence of your reading was noticeable throughout every composition.[12]

Recognizing that her stories needed refinement and revision, Sherwood decided to make the next several months profitable for professional growth, and she almost immediately undertook to cultivate the friendship of those who would best be in a position to advance her career. Therefore, during her first winter in Boston, Sherwood Bonner was bold and brash enough to write to Longfellow, already a deeply revered poet, to request a meeting, the unforeseen result of which was to initiate a deepening friendship that was to last until Longfellow's death.

Boston, Dec. 8th 1873

Dear Mr. Longfellow,
I am a Southern girl away from my home and friends. I have come here for mental discipline and study—and to try to find out the meaning and the

use of my life. It would be to me a great happiness and help if I might know you. May I come and see you please? and if so will you appoint a day and hour?

With deep respect,
Katharine Bonner[13]

address, 27 Rutland St.

Unfortunately, Longfellow's reply does not exist, but the initial meeting must have been a satisfying one to both parties, since Sherwood Bonner's position as the poet's amanuensis was shortly assured.

Relatively little is known about the following six or seven months that Sherwood Bonner spent in Boston, but much can be surmised. Nahum Capen had written Sherwood's father on October 12, 1873, that his daughter was enrolled in a Boston public school for young women and that she was at the time "pursuing her studies with great zeal and enthusiasm." One may reasonably assume that Sherwood remained in regular attendance for the remainder of that semester, if not for the remainder of the school year. Bonner, who worshipped Capen, would not have done anything either to displease her literary mentor or to suggest ingratitude. In a letter written to Ruth on November 13, 1873, Sherwood indicated her esteem for Capen:

I think if ever a saint lived upon earth it is Mr. Capen. I could fill page after page telling you of instances of his generosity and unselfishness that have come to my knowledge—and when he came to examine my religious beliefs I found that we agreed exactly. I only wish you could hear him talk; for his head is quite equal to his heart—he rarely goes to church—but the preachers all think him a saint-like old man—and so he is—my ideal of a *philosopher*.[14]

At the same time, Sherwood Bonner also recognized both the meagerness of her own training and the cold reality of the fact that her stories were simply not yet good enough for acceptance in the periodicals of the day. Despite the fact that she had read "everything in town," in addition to the works found in her father's library, her confidence in her own ability upon her arrival in Boston was not sufficient to allow her to ignore the advice of Capen, her benefactor.[15]

Apart from her schooling and the revisions of her stories, Sherwood Bonner did little of consequence during these early months in

Boston. Without exception, the four earlier biographers of Sherwood Bonner declare that she supported herself in these first few months by writing for Southern newspapers accounts of life in the North and articles describing meetings and interviews with some of New England's public figures, such as Longfellow, Wendell Phillips, Howells, and Ralph Waldo Emerson. However, the only such paper specifically mentioned by these biographers is the *Avalanche* of Memphis, Tennessee. The earliest article located in the files of the *Avalanche* appeared on Tuesday, May 4, 1875; and it describes the Lexington-Concord Centennial celebration which occurred almost eighteen months after Bonner's arrival in Boston.[16]

This brief summary of Sherwood Bonner's early months in Boston is not meant to suggest that these days were not important to her developing career. She had already met Longfellow; and by June, 1874, she had established a casual and informal correspondence with the poet. His friendship meant much in the months immediately ahead, and his early endorsement of her work gained for Sherwood Bonner entrance to editor's offices undoubtedly denied to others who were not fortunate enough to have a well-known man of letters for their personal literary advisor.

From Sherwood Bonner's first absence from Boston to the death of Longfellow, she maintained a steady correspondence with the poet. These letters, now part of the Longfellow Collection at Houghton Library, furnish a most detailed account of Bonner's productive years and supply the facts not only about her many moves during the next ten years but also about the details of her return visits to Holly Springs. One such visit took place in the early summer of 1874 when Sherwood had been in Boston less than a year. Her letter, written to Longfellow from Holly Springs on June 14, 1874, is not especially noteworthy for its content; but it indicates that the Longfellow-Bonner correspondence was not a one-sided affair, for she is obviously answering a letter recently received from the poet.

In her reply, Sherwood anticipates her return to Boston with the comment that "my Boston friends have all been so kind to me since I left that I really feel that I am going back home." That she intends to return shortly to Boston is also suggested by the statement that "I must wait until I see you to tell you how glad I was to receive your letter. From beginning to end it was just what I should have desired and made me very happy in its assurance of your continued remembrance." The remainder of the letter recounts the reception that Sherwood had been accorded by her daughter Lilian, then two years old, who "knew her at sight"; and it closes with the remark that she is eagerly looking forward to returning to Boston and resuming her literary career.

In the fall of 1874, following her return during the late summer to Boston from Holly Springs, Sherwood Bonner again acknowledges her debt to Longfellow. In her letter of November 8, 1874, written from her residence in Boston, she thanks Longfellow for "the ticket to the Radical Club. . . . You are always so good and kind." Additional evidence of the entré enjoyed by Sherwood Bonner at this time is her request for permission to bring her visitor from Kentucky, a Miss Young, to Longfellow's home: "I know among the pleasures of my friend's visit, there will be none she will value so much as a visit to your beautiful home." On Friday of that same week, a brief note from Bonner thanks the poet for the gracious hospitality he had shown both to "my friend and myself" and also informs him that she is to visit shortly in Cambridge with Mrs. John T. Sargent and that the two will call on the poet "at half-past ten or eleven" on the morning of the appointed day.

The winter of 1874–75 was a busy one for Sherwood, for she was moving closer to the initial publication of one of her local-color stories that was in turn to lead to a steady demand for such work. Still under the joint sponsorship of Capen and Longfellow and undoubtedly attempting to follow the suggestions of Dwight and other critics and editors to whom she had sent stories, Sherwood Bonner was rewriting and reediting her earlier work, preparatory to launching her formal literary career. One of Bonner's early biographers notes that the already popular writer Louisa May Alcott assisted Sherwood in her early attempts.[17]

On May 4, 1875, Sherwood Bonner's first article-letter to a Southern newspaper was published. Entitled "The Big Celebration: An *Avalanche* Correspondent's Impressions of the Lexington-Concord Centennial," the article filled three full columns with a narration of the principal events. The account reveals Bonner's natural attraction to the satirical vein; for, in describing the crowd that joined in the celebration at each city, she wrote "Judges, Governors and Senators were as plentiful as grasshoppers in either place. At both places the visitors were frozen and wretched; at both the coffee was cold and the turkey tough." The morning itself was "as cold as

Christmas snows could have made it." A splendid example of Sherwood Bonner's facile style and satiric bent is shown by her description of the making of a hero:

Acton, indeed, in her celebration struck upon a grandly original idea. Her favorite hero is Capt. Issac Davis, who was killed on the memorable 19th of April. This young butcher said on his deathbed that he started out with forty bullets, and hadn't one left; that he 'had never done such a morning's work in his life'—a boast of which his descendants are mighty proud. By way of celebration the Acton folks dug up Captain Issac, and after shedding tears over his dry bones—which suggested Mark Twain weeping at the grave of Adam—they put the sacred remains in a fresh coffin and had a grand funeral. It must have been pathetic. And it opens up endless possibilities, in the way of national holidays and celebrations.

Every family for that matter might have an entertainment of its own at any time simply by digging up its most famous ancestor.

Of more interest than the reinterment of Captain Davis, however, is Sherwood Bonner's sketch of two of the leading literary personalities of the nineteenth century—Ralph Waldo Emerson and James Russell Lowell:

The people jumped up on the benches to see their beloved philosopher, and were gratified by a sight of the tall figure (now stooping slightly, for he is over 70 years of age) and the shrewd, yet benignant face. . . .

James Russell Lowell was next introduced as 'The Poet of Cambridge and Concord.' He is a handsome man, with full, light whiskers, piercing eyes and florid complexion. We presume his poem was fine, though we heard none of it, owing to an irreverent band outside playing 'Mulligan Guards,' and noise at the edge of the tent which every moment grew more uproarious.

The remainder of the article describes the impressive homes of Concord and the receptions and dinners held throughout the day. Sherwood Bonner concludes with the dry commentary that the passing of another hundred years will see a repetition of the day with "Poets, statesmen, and orators yet unborn" thinking "the same thoughts" and uttering "the same words."

Four days after the Centennial celebration, the Boston *Sunday Times* published on May 8, 1875, Sherwood Bonner's first poem, "The Radical Club," a parody of Edgar Allan Poe's "The Raven" and a sharp satirization of the pompous Radical Club of Boston.[18] The

poem was immensely popular among Bostonians who felt that the
staid, sedate, and overly serious members of the club fully deserved
being made the laughing stock of the city.[19] The poem remained in
such wide vogue throughout that year that it was reissued in pam-
phlet form in 1876 and was reprinted upon the anniversary of its
original publication in 1877 by the original publisher.[20]

On the last Sunday of the same month, May 30, 1875, Bonner's
second article for the Memphis *Avalanche* appeared; datelined May
19, it was entitled "Wendell Phillips: Interviewed by a Southern
Girl." Sherwood Bonner's sharp eye for detail missed nothing either
in Phillips' home or in the interview itself, which lasted for an hour
and a half. She describes his desk as a "mahogany table covered with
papers, books and manuscripts in a most chaotic disorder." There
are no pictures on the wall, and no "tokens of luxury." There were
three busts: one of a relative; one of "John Brown, whom Mr. Phillips regards as a saint"; and a third of himself. "The books were
mostly on governmental and social science—by Spencer, Mill, De-
Tocqueville and that sort of fellows, for whom men seem to have the
same perverse taste that shows itself in their consumption of cigars
and love and lager beer and politics and other similar abomina-
tions." The bulk of the interview dealt with Reconstruction and with
the future of the South, a future which Phillips maintained de-
pended largely on Northern industrial expansion to the South and,
therefore, primarily on Northern capital. The article is noteworthy
for Sherwood Bonner's estimate of Wendell Phillips, and in it she
classifies and separates critics and creators. Phillips' chief limitation,
Bonner thought, was that "he is a critic, not a creator. His personal
influence will end with his generation. It may have been great, but
it must have been rather negative than positive. The Cassandras
have never saved a country yet. . . . the critic is always and always
has been overestimated as an intellectual force in his life
time. . . . The 'everlasting no' gets monotonous in the long run."

The following month another of the *Avalanche* letters, "Boston's
Centennial: A Southern Woman's Description of the Celebration at
Bunker Hill," was published. The letter, datelined June 18, 1875,
appeared in the June 13 issue. A lengthy letter, it describes the
week's events of the Centennial, which began with the opening of
an exhibition house on famed Beacon Street; at this ceremony,
Oliver Wendell Holmes read his poem, 'Grandmother's Story,' with a

pathos and fire that went to every heart." A catalog-description follows of the principal items exhibited.

One of the highlights of the week-long celebration, at least to Sherwood Bonner, was the warmth and sincerity of the affectionate greeting shown by the people of Boston to the Southern marching units in the Centennial parade. The two hundred thousand visitors who poured through every street in Boston, the general air of gaiety, and the heartwarming strains of "Dixie" and "Maryland, My Maryland" combined to produce in everyone "a feeling of joyous enthusiasm." The parade itself was evidence of the public participation in the celebration, for over fifty thousand marchers made a line seven miles long. Perhaps the most interesting and touching sight in the parade was the presence of two of the opposing generals of the Civil War. Not surprisingly, both were equally revered: "The greatest enthusiasm was reserved for Sherman and Lee. Sherman seemed delighted with the universal fire, threw kisses to the children and responded in every possible way to the eager demonstrations. Lee stood up in his carriage, his head uncovered—a gallant figure—and bowed with courtly grace." Sherwood Bonner had herself never held any animosity toward the North after the defeat of the Southern cause, and it is therefore not surprising that she concludes her description of Boston's Centennial by expressing the "conviction that a new era had begun—a conciliation to which we might point the world with pride . . . and which holds substantial promise of a prosperous future for our once more united country."

A little over two months after the publication of "The Radical Club" and less than thirty days after the third of the *Avalanche* articles appeared, Sherwood Bonner published her first local-color story and began her formal literary career. The story, written in rough form as early as 1873, appeared in the July 29, 1875, edition of the *Youth's Companion* and was entitled "Gran'mammy's Last Gifts." It was appropriate that Sherwood Bonner's literary career began with a story in which her much beloved gran'mammy was the principal character.

Seven weeks later, on September 18, 1875, Sherwood wrote to her father, from Boston, that she was "going Saturday with Mr. Longfellow to call on Mr. Howells, the Editor of the *Atlantic Monthly* and author of those charming books, *Their Wedding Journey* and *A Chance Acquaintance.* He is a man I've long wanted to meet, and I'm all in a flutter of delighted anticipation. Have had my black silk fixed short and will get some fawn colored gloves and new bonnet strings and curl my hair. Hope to strike his majesty favorably, tho I hear he's a stern business man, and I hope I may be very much impressed as it takes one nail to drive out another."[21] Whatever the outcome of this particular meeting, it did not result in the acceptance, then or later, of any of Sherwood Bonner's writings. Nevertheless, it is important to her developing career, in view of the Realism of her later work, to point out that she knew early of the pioneer Realism of Howells and Henry James.

In October, only a few weeks after her visit to Howells, Sherwood Bonner again returned to Holly Springs, primarily to see her daughter Lilian. On November 2, 1875, she wrote to Longfellow informing him that she would return to Boston on "the ninth or tenth of November" and would be accompanied by her sister Ruth. Sherwood added that the two would be staying with the Nahum Capen family in Dorchester, a few miles from Boston; and she requested Longfellow to prevail upon Edith, his daughter, to call upon Ruth in order to make Ruth feel more at home. Exactly two weeks later Sherwood Bonner wrote Longfellow from Mt. Ida, Capen's home, to ask if she should bring Ruth to Cambridge or if she should first "make a 'business call' alone and receive instructions about the work I look forward to with so much pleasure!" The note concludes, familiarly and affectionately, "Ruth . . . is delighted at the thought of seeing you in your beautiful home—and I—I have a thousand things to say to you. . . ."[22]

The work about which Bonner was to receive instructions from Longfellow concerned her services to him in the compilation and editing of his projected series, *Poems of Places* (1876). Consequently, the following three months were among the busiest that Sherwood Bonner ever experienced. Although no actual work was performed by Sherwood on *Poems of Places* until after her tour of Europe, conferences were held at the poet's home in Cambridge as preparation for the role that Sherwood was to play. That the young Southern writer was already a frequent visitor to Longfellow's home is suggested by her fourth *Avalanche* article, "Sherwood Bonner's Letter: Longfellow's Home—Its History," which appeared on December 26, 1875. The article begins by tracing the history of the home, which had been built around the middle of the eighteenth century by Colonel John Yassal and which had at one time been occupied by George Washington. The interesting observation is made that Longfellow first lived in the home as a lodger while a "young Professor at Harvard College." At that time, the home was owned by a Mrs. Craigie from whom Longfellow bought it in 1843. Regrettably, no special attention is paid to any single room, neither to the library nor to Longfellow's study; the entire article, with the exception of the last three brief paragraphs, is a detailed description of the house and grounds.

The tone of these concluding paragraphs is one of reverence and admiration. Sherwood Bonner undoubtedly had her own debt to the poet in mind, and perhaps her initial reception by him when she wrote that "The young poet who goes to Longfellow need not fear a cold reception or an indifferent listener. Genuine sympathy he will surely find; and should his verses hold one glimmer of the sacred fire, just that wise encouragement for want of which Keats died and Chatterton 'perished in his pride.' " The last comment is of some incidental interest because it not only indicates that Sherwood Bonner had read Shelley and Wordsworth but also suggests that Shelley's opinion as the cause of Keats' death was still currently held by some admirers of Keats.

II *Widening Horizons: England, Paris, Rome, and Return*

At about the same time that Bonner was preparing to be the amanuensis of Longfellow, her own writing career was progressing rather swiftly. In December, 1875, the short story "Miss Willard's Two Rings" appeared in *Lippincott's Magazine*—her first publication in a serious literary periodical. Less than a month later, in the January 6, 1876, issue of *Youth's Companion*, appeared the second of her local-color stories, "Gran'mammy's Story" (renamed "The Night the Stars Fell" in the *Suwanee River Tales* collection). Almost simultaneously with the publication of these stories, Sherwood Bonner announced a six-month tour of Europe to commence on January 22, 1876; for she had obtained contracts from both the Memphis *Avalanche* and the Boston *Times* to publish a series of letter-articles describing her reactions to Europe. For these articles she was to receive ten dollars a letter from each newspaper, a sum which she felt would support her during her sojourn abroad.[23] Her traveling companion during the greater part of the tour was Louise Chandler Moulton, a highly popular reviewer and poet.[24]

In preparation for her European tour, Bonner wrote in mid-

January to Longfellow from Capen's home in Dorchester that she would come to Cambridge "early Tuesday morning for the letter [of introduction] you so kindly promised me." Five days later Sherwood Bonner left for New York, where she was to meet Mrs. Moulton. Since the *Baltic*, the ship on which the two were to sail to England, did not leave until the twenty-third, Sherwood had approximately four days in New York to devote to making new acquaintances among Mrs. Moulton's circle of friends. One of the literary lights that she recalls having met at this time was E. C. Stedman, whose *Victorian Poets* she had found "exquisite." The letter containing this account, started in New York prior to the sailing of the *Baltic*, was concluded on the first of February as the ship neared Liverpool. The content, somewhat dated and tiresome, consists primarily of dinnertime conversation with and about other passengers and of observations of the differences between British and American tourists. The letter was published as a one and a half column article in the Sunday *Avalanche* on February 27 under the headline-title "Sherwood Bonner: An *Avalanche* Correspondent's Voyage Across the Atlantic."

Two days before the docking of the *Baltic* at Liverpool, Sherwood wrote a second letter, this one to Longfellow. In it, she describes the appearance of several of the other passengers, the table talk of her dining room companions, and the roughness of the voyage. She remarks coyly that Longfellow will be happy to know that she was not seasick a single time, despite some extremely bad weather. This letter, written on January 30, is typical of the chatty, informal rambling letters that Sherwood Bonner frequently addressed to Longfellow when she was away from the immediate vicinity of Boston and Cambridge.

The letters to Longfellow, detailing her travels and describing her itinerary, continued to be regular. She wrote him from Paris on February 10, narrating an account of a shopping trip and the delights of dining in Paris. Sherwood was greatly impressed at the reasonable prices in Paris, especially in comparison with those that she and Mrs. Moulton had encountered in London. She wrote the poet from Rome on March 5 to thank him not only for his letter to her but more especially for the care and attention he had showered upon "little Ruthie." Bonner was even more impressed with Rome than she had been with Paris: "Every day the charm of this wonderful old city deepens. I should never tire of it. It is an enchantment to be here." She concludes the letter with an account of her birthday party and of the joyous time that she and Mrs. Moulton had "exploring quaint old places in the morning, cameo shops in the afternoon—and cameo shops here are galleries of art."

Between her letters to Longfellow, she wrote the newspaper accounts of her travels for the *Avalanche* and the *Times*. On March 15, the *Avalanche* published "Sherwood Bonner: A Southern Woman's Impressions of England and the English," which was datelined Charing Cross Hotel, February 10. More than half of this article concerns her criticism of the dress of the English, especially the women. The London theater receives its share of attention, and Sherwood and Mrs. Moulton saw *All for Her*, based upon Dickens' *A Tale of Two Cities*, at the St. James Theatre. They also saw Genevieve Ward as Lady Macbeth, and were greatly impressed with the strength of her performance.

Judging from Bonner's enthusiastic description, however, the principal highlight of their stay in London was witnessing the scene in the House of Lords when Queen Victoria "opened Parliament for the first time in five years." Since wild rumors and reports had circulated that "she was about to abdicate and give up the reins of government to the Prince of Wales," her address was much awaited by the people. Bonner enjoyed the pageantry of the occasion, but she was disappointed in the appearance and plainness of the queen. In an obvious paraphrase of the opening lines of "Endymion," Bonner notes that "The Royal Lady may be a joy forever to the British heart, but certainly she is not a thing of beauty. . . . She was a plain center to her brilliant surroundings; a sort of soap-stone set in diamonds." Sherwood, shocked by the behavior of the members of Parliament, remarked that, "when the Commons were called[,] that unruly body came in, in a most tumultuous fashion. They jostled and hustled poor Mr. Disraeli until he withdrew in disgust." Her descriptions and tone remind one of the irreverent attitude of Mark Twain in *Innocents Abroad*, for her comments are refreshingly frank when she satirizes or ridicules the usual tourist attractions. This particular letter concludes with an account of the ceremonial procession, enacted with all the pomp traditionally associated with such august events, when queen left Parliament.

Shortly after witnessing the queen's appearance in Parliament, Sherwood and Mrs. Moulton continued their European tour, going first to Paris, thence to Rome, then to Florence. While in Florence, Sherwood Bonner received the following letter from Longfellow, the only complete letter of his to Bonner that survives:

Cambridge
February 27, 1876

Dear Aurora:

Today is my birthday as perhaps you remember, but I shall not tell you whether I am sixty nine or ninety six.

I sit here surrounded by beautiful flowers, sent by sympathetic friends. I wish I could send some of them to you in Rome, but as Rome is the land of flowers, it would be like sending "Owls to Athens" which is Greek for "Coals to Newcastle." But of all these flowers none are as sweet as your dear rambling letter from Paris, the place to which the good Bostonians go when they die. It came this morning with the other bouquets, and made me very happy. It reminds me of Grey's description of Lady Coleham's house at Stoke Poges, having "Rich windows that exclude the light, and passages that lead to nothing," nothing I mean but what is charming and pleasant to remember.

Write me always in this way, and fear no criticism from me, and write as often as you can, nor a moment think that it can be too often. I rejoice in your happiness, and am thankful that it has gone so well with you,—I only wish I could be your cicerone in Rome. Nine months of my youth I lived in a house fronting on the Plaza Navona. Do not fail to tell me where you have your lodgings. It is always a pleasure to know where one's friends are, and imagine what they first see when they go out of doors, and what they always see when they look out of their windows.

The Poems of Places in which you have aided me so much, and will aid me on your return, "Drags its slow length along"—I never could or would have believed it such an endless task—Luckily it is a pleasure to live with the poets.

And now Dear Aurora I hear the "Bells of Shandon" ringing and they say "With deep affection, and recollection."

Henry W. Longfellow[25]

Sherwood Bonner's reply to this letter was not written until the middle of April when Longfellow's letter finally reached her in Florence. "I have just read your kind and dear letter, which I found awaiting me like a friendly hand. I am selfish enough to be glad you miss me. I am already beginning to dream of home." She continues to praise Rome lavishly: "I was so happy in Rome. No other place in the world can ever so completely fill my soul. The longer I stayed the deeper the fascination grew—and I am afraid I cried when I left it. I was glad you told me where you lived in Rome. I wish I had known the house. I used to try sometimes to imagine what Rome would have been with you to show it to me and tell me about things—but I suppose it is not given to mortals to know perfect bliss." She remarks that she has been able to do some work and had completed "three letters for the *Times* and *Avalanche*," but she laments that there has been no time to write stories. The letter concludes, "—Goodnight—It is better to dream than to write— Yours, K."[26]

The *Avalanche* letters to which she alluded in this letter were written between February 22 and June 18; and almost all of them relate to her lengthy stay in Rome. The *Avalanche* for March 26 published the article "Sherwood Bonner: Southern Woman's Trip from London to Rome" (datelined Rome, February 22). Bonner and Mrs. Moulton had spent only two days in Paris before departing by steamer from Marseilles for Genoa, where they spent one day awaiting passage to Rome. Their Roman visit lasted five full weeks, and each day in Rome was an experience in itself. On the day following their arrival, they visited the Protestant Cemetery at Rome for the unveiling of a memorial medallion of John Keats in honor of the fifty-fifth anniversary of his death. Incredible as it may seem, Joseph Severn, then eighty-three, was still residing in Rome; but he was not present at the ceremonies honoring Keats since "it was feared the agitation of the scene might be too much for him." The letter closes with the sad observation that both Shelley "and the only child of Shelley and Mary Wollstoncraft—a boy of three," were also buried in the same cemetery, and Bonner laments "the fate that pursues so many gifted souls!"

The next *Avalanche* letter, published in the Sunday, April 9, edition, describes "Rome's Carnival: Sherwood Bonner's Description of Carnival Week in the Eternal City." The title indicates the contents, Rome's Mardi Gras celebration, complete with parades and midnight balls. The conclusion of the letter reveals again Bonner's gift for satire and humor. In it she gives an account of Rome's principal nuisances: (1) fleas, "as plentiful as leaves," "as fleet as darting sunbeams," "as stinging as a Southern editor"; (2) the flower girls, or "violet-girls. They are of all ages, from six to sixty, and they besiege you like an army of gnats"; and, finally, (3) the "people who pity us. These are the English and American residents who tell us, with a superior air, that five weeks are nothing to give to Rome." They "rail at Mark Twain, and groan over the fact that the demand for the 'Innocents Abroad' is so great that it is actually sold here as a guide book." The nuisances notwithstanding, Sherwood Bonner concludes that "Rome is the most fascinating place in the world."

The article for April 30, "Sherwood Bonner: An *Avalanche* Correspondent's Visit to the Pope," continues in the satirical vein of Bonner's description of Queen Victoria at Parliament. In this letter she presents a humorous summation of the instructions given to those desirous of obtaining an audience with the pope: "We were to kneel when His Holiness appeared; kneel and kiss his hand when he spoke to us; kneel when he went out; smile if he smiled; weep if he wept; bear ourselves in all things as became the satellites around so mighty a planet." The "interview" was no more than a general audience, and Bonner's description of it is in the tradition of Twain's in *Innocents Abroad:* "Like Rip, he blessed not only ourselves, but our families; further yet our clothes, our ornaments, everything about us. (Even the little flea skipping airily across my shoulder became at that moment a blessed flea.)" Sherwood concludes that "Rome is the last place for a heretic to be brought back to the fold of the Mother Church; for with all of the interest pertaining to the spectacular religion, it excites wonder rather than reverence."

The next two letters, published two weeks apart in the *Avalanche* (the first on May 14; the second on May 28), continue her description of Rome. Neither is so carefully prepared as the earlier letters, and both are rambling and inconsequential. The last letter written from Rome describes Easter Sunday Mass at St. Peters and the brilliant Roman countryside: "How beautiful it is! How far beyond painting of word or brush!"[27] Clearly, Sherwood Bonner's interest in, and enthusiasm for, Rome began to wane after she had been there several weeks and she and her companion had seen the principal sights.

From Rome, the two continued to Florence, where they spent an entire week. The one letter from Florence, entitled "Beautiful Florence: The Art Galleries of the Birthplace of Michael Angelo," which appeared in the *Avalanche* on July 9, contains the typical tourist's inspection of, and commentary about, the usual tourist attractions. In Venice, however, Sherwood Bonner regained the satiric touch that had heightened the appeal of her earliest European tour letters. The article, "At Venice: Sherwood Bonner Visits the 'Bride of the Sea' and is Happy," datelined Venice, May, 1876, did not appear in the *Avalanche* until August 6; and in it Bonner recounts the activities of the four days that she and Mrs. Moulton had spent in Venice, as well as their trip to Verona. The principal attraction of Verona was the tomb of Juliet, and Sherwood Bonner's description of her visit to it reveals again Twain's influence. The scene closely parallels Twain's treatment of his Italian guide in Rome:

> Just outside the walls on the road to the old monastery, we were accosted by a black-eyed boy who offered . . . to show us the tomb of Guiletta. Desirous of making the youngster earn his centimes, I assumed a vacant stare, and said, 'Guiletta! Who was she?'
>
> 'Ah, Signora! Guiletta—Romero—' he repeated vaguely.
>
> 'What did they do?' inquired I, in a prosaic tone.
>
> He rolled his dark eyes heavenward and said they were lovers.
>
> 'Lovers? Indeed! Very improper. Did they ever marry?'
>
> 'No, no, signora. They died. They were very unhappy.' And then with precocity beyond his years he poured forth the story in a manner that proved him of the poet's opinion:
>
> > 'Never was a story of more woe
> > Than this of Juliet and her Romeo.'

Soon after their excursion to Verona, Mrs. Moulton and Bonner returned to Paris where they remained for the better part of the summer of 1876. From Paris, Bonner wrote on May 30 to Longfellow that, although she still loved all of Paris almost as much as she had Rome, lately "the object of my exclusive devotion here is the skating rink." She then describes the pleasant afternoons spent at the rink, where she learned both the art of skating and that of French conversation.

On August 8, 1876, Sherwood Bonner wrote to her sister Ruth, implying her return to America in the near future, and outlining her plans: "I will surely go to Philadelphia with you and then may rush home for two weeks and back again in order to see about a book that I want to get out by the Xmas. holidays—a juvenile collection of my short stories and one longer I have just finished—and also to help Mr. Longfellow finish his book—then I shall go back home and pitch into my novel heart and soul.[28]

In late August, 1876, Sherwood Bonner returned to Boston. In a letter to her father, written in mid-October and now in the possession of David McDowell, she implies that she has been in Dorches-

ter with the Capen family for several days; and she enlarges upon
the plans she had previously outlined to Ruth in one of her last
letters from Paris:

                                                Boston, Oct. 16th, '76
Dear Father;
    I have been safe at Mt. Ida for some days now, but as yet haven't had
much rest—go out to Mr. Longfellow's nearly every day. It seems to me
really that I shall never have sleep enough—expect to devote myself to it
when I get home. I have not quite decided upon my future movements. I
want to do what is right with regard to Edward and have written him that I
will go with him to Galveston, but on the other hand I have promised Mr.
Longfellow to do this work, and as it is impossible to finish it before I leave
it almost seems that I am in honor bound to come back. Still I would rather
not do so. If I am ever to go to Galveston, this seems to be the time. I might
go to Philadelphia with Ruth in November, spend a few days there and
come back to Boston. But that hardly seems worth while for the few weeks
before Christmas, and I cannot make up my mind to stay longer without
going home. I can't miss the fatted calf feast even if it is a *borrowed* beast.
Stolen fruit is sweet and I suppose a borrowed calf would be particularly
toothsome. I don't know I am sure what Edward will say to my coming
back. Probably it would be a good idea to go to Galveston with E. in
January, stay until May, then come North and take up Mr. L's work again
having at the same time the ms. of the book ready to read to him. However,
there's no use worrying about this matter now. It will arrange itself. . . . I
am getting pretty homesick for Auntee and Lilian. I expect to find my little
one so much grown that I will hardly know her. I wish I had *her* and a home
here in Boston. It seems a great pity to leave now when my literary prospects are so bright. The Editor of the *Times* is very anxious for me to form a
permanent connection with his paper—he says the circulation has largely
increased since I began to write for it—and the other night at a reception
another Editor told me that I had already made a name—that my future was
assured, etc. . . .
    Four volumes of Mr. Longfellow's book are out and it is meeting with
great success. There will be some fifteen volumes—work enough to keep
me busy for a year if I choose to take it. He is *so* kind to me—better and
better all the time. . . .

In addition to the work that Sherwood was doing for Longfellow on
the multivolume *Poems of Places*, she was also completing and revising her next two short stories; and each was suggested by events that
had occurred during her stay in Paris. "Rosine's Story" appeared in

the *Youth's Companion* for December 14, 1876; and "Leonie" was also published in the *Youth's Companion* on February 8, 1877.

True to her announced intentions in the October 16 letter to her father, Christmas of 1876 found Sherwood Bonner once again in Holly Springs. Between October and December of that year, she had been almost wholly occupied with her work on *Poems of Places*. In the Bonner-Longfellow correspondence two of her notes (dated only with the year 1876) apologize for not having kept appointments with the poet, and for thereby missing "the usual happy hours in your study." Since Bonner had been in Europe from January through August, 1876, the notes obviously belong to the last few months of that year. As was her custom whenever she was separated from Longfellow by any considerable distance, Sherwood wrote to the poet from Holly Springs on Christmas Day of 1876 in the warmest terms as she narrated the difficulties of her long journey to Holly Springs and the details of the affectionate welcome that had awaited her at home. This letter also concludes with a tantalizing final paragraph: "Please write me a *real* letter—ah! you won't have an amanuensis to answer *this* for you! Tell me of the work—if you miss me—if you sleep well—and if you have what my baby calls 'sweet kind thoughts,' of her who loves you so well."[29]

Immediately after the Christmas holidays, Sherwood Bonner returned to Boston, primarily to assist Longfellow in the *Poems of Places* project and to begin work on her already projected novel. On March 3, 1877, she wrote to Ruth from Boston of her intention to delay her reunion with Edward in Galveston, Texas:

You will understand why I want to stay here a while longer. Perhaps in addition to other reasons it will be well to give poor Edward a little longer chance of establishing himself at something.

He writes to me no more, but in his last letter he told me that his uncle's affairs were desperate, and that he knew not where to turn. Total weakness! Fatal lack of purpose! To think of the years one after another that have followed since I first knew him—each one more barren of results than the last.[30]

Three days later she wrote to Ruth to tell her about a sociable that she had given in honor of "Modjeska, the great Polish actress." A large number of prominent persons were in attendance, including "Mr. Longfellow, of course, and his brothers-in-law, the Appletons, very swell fellows. . . . Modjeska is lovely and charming, every inch a countess, but the noble count, her husband, is a tall, wiggling sort of man, looking like a snake standing on its tail."[31] In this letter to Ruth, Sherwood made no mention of Edward and Galveston.

The following week, however, on March 11, Sherwood Bonner wrote a six-page letter to Longfellow from Holly Springs in which she announced several present and future events. First, and perhaps most importantly of all, she told the poet that she would definitely be leaving for Galveston on the following Friday and since she would spend a week in New Orleans on the way, she urged Longfellow to write her there. Second, she thanked the poet for sending her "the Boston papers and the Atlantic" and expressed her anticipation of the French volume of *Poems of Places* which Longfellow had already sent to her but which she had not yet received. Third, she conveyed the news of Ruth's marriage, to take place sometime after Easter, as "Ruth has decided it a sin to be married in Lent, so the wedding will not be until after Easter." The letter closed "Gratefully and lovingly yours," and for the first time Sherwood signed the letter with the initials "KSB." All of her other letters to Longfellow had used either the McDowell name or initial in the closing signature.

On April 17, she wrote Longfellow from Galveston to thank him for the letter from him which she found upon her arrival, and she notes that she had now been in Galveston for two weeks. She again thanks the poet for the papers and periodicals he continues to send to her, especially for "the French paper. I read the article about Victor Hugo with so much interest. How I should like to have a good introduction into the literary society of Paris." She adds that she intends to take French lessons from a New Orleans native while in Galveston and that she manages to read a little each day in either one of the two books by Molière she had brought with her or in "the Rousseau Confessions" which she has found at the local library. She notes finally that Ruth is to marry her husband's brother, David McDowell, on April 28.

The next letter to Longfellow, undated, announces the beginning of the novel: "*The Work* is at last begun! One chapter is written." In an obvious reference to Longfellow's suggestion that the setting of her first novel be Boston,[32] Sherwood wrote the poet that "it seems to be better to make the book purely Southern; so the scene is to be laid in Virginia and Louisiana." Sherwood adds that she has now commenced her French lessons under a Mr. Coryin and is delighted with her progress. Again she alludes to the books, papers, and periodicals he has sent, and she reassures him that he can't send too many: "No, indeed you do not send too many books and papers. I am so glad to get them. I read them with great interest—and they come to me like friendly tokens." In an interesting comment on her reaction to present-day Realism, she observes that she has just received "the May number of the Atlantic—and am in despair at the wretched and unsatisfactory close of Mr. James' story, 'The American.'" Despite her initial reaction to James and his brand of Realism, Bonner was to move more and more away from mere local color toward the then newly emerging Realism.

On May 7, two months after her letter to Longfellow announcing her initial work on the novel, Sherwood wrote to the editor of the *Cottage Hearth*, a Mr. Millikin, about her novel and recalled former pleasures of life in Boston:

How do things get on in dear old Boston. The Cottage Hearth I know gets on well. I think every number better than the last. . . .

Now I will tell you a little of myself. After much debate and deliberation here I am in this inland city—living in the most orthodox, conventional style—a century away from the little room of three flights on Tremont Pl. where I had such good times with you clever men dropping in with fresh gossip and witticisms and a breezy air of work. Galveston is . . . on a sand bar—is all overrun with oleander trees and rose-bushes now in full bloom. From my window I watch the sea all day, and in the afternoon I walk or drive on the finest beach in the United States. Don't think all this means that I have given up literary work. No indeed—I was never so ambitious—and—here is a grand piece of news—I have really *begun my novel!* The scene is to be laid in Virginia, and I expect to go there this summer to study up localities, characters, and Md. family records. Sometimes I am hopeful of grand success—at others I am very despondent. Give me a word of cheer won't you? I know I may count on your sympathy.[33]

Her plans to go to Virginia for the summer to undertake research work for her novel never materialized, and she implies as early as mid-June in a letter to Longfellow that, for the present at least, she intends to remain with Edward in Galveston. The only mention of the novel is one about her fear that her ability is not sufficient to allow her to complete an acceptable work.[34] In July, while still in Galveston, she wrote an optimistic but guarded note to Ruth in which she again implies that she had no intention of leaving Edward in the immediate future: "Edward has written often what he knows—which is not very much. But he is deeply interested and will do *all* that he can. Heaven grant that our guano may come to something. The first shipment is off, but it is not yet time to hear from it. If you could see the letters he is constantly getting from reliable business men at the north—men who wouldn't *look* at the thing unless they saw money—you would feel assured of a success. Mr. Goodridge says it's a fortune, but he may be over sanguine."[35]

Despite the implication in her letter to Ruth that she and Edward would remain together—especially with the reference to "our guano"—on August 31 she wrote a long letter to Longfellow from Holly Springs summarizing her summer's work. She has now given her novel a title, but she admits having done little actual work on it: "I fear you will lose patience with me when I tell you that 'The Prodigal Daughter' has been no part of my summer's work. It was no use. I *had* to rid my mind of these Southern stories before I could do anything else."[36] She adds that her husband has consented to her return North, "chiefly on Lilian's account." Edward, who felt that the Northern educational system was superior to that of the South, wanted Lilian to have every educational advantage. She also remarked that several of her friends were begging her to come to New York City; but, "while there is one heart left to care for me in Boston," she intended to return to it.

In the same letter she lamented the fact that "My homecoming has been the saddest I have ever known," primarily because her favorite, Ruth, now married, was no longer at home. She also mentioned that her father has frequently spoken about selling "Bonner House" and the adjacent plantation and about moving to the Pacific coast, an event that would prove a doubly sad occasion for Sherwood. She did not wish her father to move such a distance, and she did not like to think about "Bonner House" falling into the hands of a stranger while she still lived. Dr. Bonner did nothing about selling either the house or land, and Sherwood Bonner remained in Holly Springs for the next six weeks.

On October 10 she wrote to Longfellow from Memphis to advise him that she was spending a few days with Lilian on vacation before returning to Boston and that she would "be in Boston before this golden month is ended," an obvious reference to the fact that October was Longfellow's favorite month. After her return North, she remained in the East for the next nine months; she spent most of her time in Boston but made occasional short trips to New York City. Although her novel was engaging more and more of her time, she still found the time to have three more of her stories published in periodicals during the next five months. The first of the three, "Breaking the News," appeared in *Youth's Companion* for December 27, 1877; this story was subsequently renamed "How Gran'mammy Broke the News" when it was collected in *Suwanee River Tales*. In the February, 1878, issue of *Lippincott's* appeared "In Aunt Mely's Cabin," another of the autobiographical Gran'mammy tales. That same month, on February 7, Sherwood Bonner wrote to Longfellow of her plans to spend the next few weeks in New York City with some of her visiting Southern friends. The third story of the period, "Dear Eyelashes," was published in *Youth's Companion* in March, 1878.

Following her return to Boston in early March, she suffered a brief period of ill health and wrote to Longfellow that she had been unable to work with any degree of dedication on her novel. She proposed a short trip to see her sister, then living in St. Louis, in order to rest and recover her health.[37] Possibly, however, she was more depressed in spirit than ill in body, for a little more than two months later, on May 18, she wrote Longfellow in the most glowing terms:

Dear, dear, dear, Mr. Longfellow—
                    The gates are opened, and heaven is mine! Like Unto Like is accepted! . . . How shall I thank you to whom I owe all.[38]

In a much longer letter to her father, written three days after her exuberant one to Longfellow, Sherwood wrote in detail of the feelings that possessed her upon the attainment of one of her fondest dreams:

My dear Father,
                    You will be delighted to hear that my book has been accepted by Harpers and with so many words of praise that my head is almost turned. I never was so flattered in my life. . . . Mr. Joseph Harper came to see me, and Mr. Alden, the Editor of the magazine . . . sent for me to come to see him, and it was he who so delighted me with his warm praise of the book. He said it was very remarkable—that it was refreshing to read a

book of so much power, freshness and originality—that it was very
artistic—that the characters were drawn with singular individuality. . . . then he compared my method with George Eliot's—said that she
dissected her characters—analyzed them chemically and from without
out—but I from without, in. . . . Then he went on to ask that I would write
for the magazine—some Southern stories. . . .

It was so late in the season that I did not dream they would publish before
fall. . . .

I do feel very proud and happy, and I am sure all those who love me will
feel the same. It is worth all the suffering I have gone through in having so
many cruel and unjust things said of me. I believe now that a great future is
possible, and I may be a rich woman too by my own exertions before I
die!. . . You never saw any one so pleased as Mr. Longfellow. He says,
"Now you see I was a fine prophet. Another time and you will have more
confidence in my judgment."[39]

III   *Lengthening Shadows: The Plague of 1878,*
Divorce, Sickness, and Death

Sherwood Bonner's joy occasioned by the publication of her first
and only novel was not destined to last the summer of 1878, for
Holly Springs, thought by its citizens to be impregnable because of
its altitude, was threatened in mid-August by the dreaded yellow
fever plague. In three months the population of the city shrank from
thirty-five hundred to fewer than fifteen hundred, and in this same
period 1440 cases of yellow fever were reported, as were 305 veri-
fiable deaths.[40] Two of those who died were Sherwood's father and
her brother. Dr. Charles Bonner had refused to leave when it was
evident that the plague was going to reach epidemic proportions, for
he realized that he would be urgently needed as a physician. His
son, Sam, elected to remain to do what he could for his father.
Sherwood Bonner left Boston on August 29, as soon as she heard of
the outbreak, to attempt to persuade her father and brother to
return North with her. By the time of her arrival in Holly Springs on
September 4, both her father and brother were stricken; and she
telegraphed Longfellow in desperation: "Help for God's sake. Send
money. Father and brother down yellow fever. Alone to nurse." On
the same date she sent Longfellow a postal card, expressing the fear
that she, too, had contracted the fever, but such a conclusion proved
premature.

Five days later, Sherwood telegraphed Longfellow from Cincinnati to announce the death of her father and brother and to ask the

poet again to send the money needed for travel since his original check had been temporarily lost with her misdirected baggage. In a second telegram of the same date from Cincinnati, Sherwood advised the poet that she had received the money and that she was doing all she could to reach Boston. The exact details of her escape from Holly Springs are not known, for all the roads leading out of Memphis, Grenanda, and New Orleans, where the plague was also rampant, were closed by a strict quarantine. One of Bonner's early biographers credits James Redpath, at that time editor of the *North American Review*, with using his considerable influence to secure permission for Sherwood Bonner to return to Boston.[41]

Although Sherwood Bonner spent less than one week in Holly Springs, she had seen enough of the terrible toll taken by the fever to enable her to compose a vivid picture of the plague-stricken town. She described the approach and presence of the fever in a lengthy article privately published in Holly Springs on February 1, 1879, entitled "A Chapter in the History of the Epidemic of 1878":

Sunday morning, August 25, 1878, was announced with the usual chime of bells, calling the worshippers to the place of prayer. That morning the bells gave out a brief warning sound, but met no glad response, and only a few devout hearts bowed in the sanctuary of the Lord. . . . The very air, which seemed so health giving, was filled with a solemn awe, and dread and unnamed fears possessed every heart, lest in the darkness of the night before, the seeds of the 'yellow death' had been sown.

In this hour of dreadful extremity, when we seemed drifting pilotless upon a sea of uncertainty and despair, a few brave men met and organized a relief committee. . . . This timely aid, together with the supplies and sympathy which began to flow in from all quarters, and with the repeated assurances of the physicians that they would soon have the disease under control, began to inspire us with new hope. But, alas! in one short week what a death list!

The plague had asserted itself throughout the entire town, and left absolute desolation in its track. By day and by night, the slow, sepulchral rumbling of the hearses greeted our ears; and, ever and anon, the physicians swiftly passed on their busy, yet hopeless rounds.

The world will never know all the horrors of this fearful visitation, which has graced with the crown of martyrdom the fairest and best of a people whose labors and lives have been given in the efforts to save others.[42]

The months after Sherwood Bonner's return to Boston were ones of feverish activity in an attempt to divert her thoughts from the recent and tragic loss of her father and brother. She found consolation and encouragement in the familiar surroundings of Longfellow's study in Cambridge, where she continued to assist the poet in his compilation of *Poems of Places*. At the same time, her own writings made regular appearances in *Harpers'*, *Lippincott's*, and the *Youth's Companion*. In September, 1878, *Lippincott's* published "C. G., or Lily's Earrings," which contained a French poem written by Longfellow especially for Bonner's story.[43] Two months later, on November 3, Sherwood joined her father's sister Martha—her "Auntee"—and her own daughter Lilian for a few days' visit with some of Martha's former acquaintances in Penn Yan, New York. In that same month she returned again to Holly Springs, leaving Lilian with Martha at Penn Yan, while Sherwood and Ruth tried to decide what to do with "Bonner House." Martha settled the matter for them when she arrived in Holly Springs with Lilian and declared that she had lived too long in "Bonner House" to call any other place home.

Sherwood Bonner remained in Holly Springs throughout the winter and early spring of 1879, writing her stories and getting reacquainted with Lilian. On April 18, she rather boldly informed Longfellow that Lilian was to be baptized the following day and that Longfellow was her daughter's choice for godfather. Sherwood apologized for "asking" Longfellow to serve, and she added that she had arranged for one of her old friends to serve as Longfellow's proxy. In the same letter, she outlined her personal objections to the baptism ceremony; but she had reluctantly decided to allow it because Lilian desired it and because her dead father and brother would have been pleased by it. Two weeks later Sherwood Bonner returned to Boston, and she notified Longfellow of her arrival in a brief note written to him from St. James Hotel, her Boston quarters.[44]

Nothing is known directly about the next two months of Sherwood Bonner's stay in Boston; but it may be assumed, on the basis of stories published during the fall of 1879 and the winter of 1880, that she was fairly busy with writing. As early as May, 1879, *St. Nicholas Magazine* published another of Bonner's numerous stories for young people, "The Terrible Adventures of Ourselves and the Marshall" (a large but friendly spider). The money she received for *Like Unto Like* and such occasional stories as "The Marshall," together with her portion of the family income from her father's estate, may have allowed her the time she had always wanted to rework and rewrite her fiction. Very likely, she was already at work during this time on a second novel or a novelette; for she wrote Longfellow in December, 1879, that she had at last finished "her long story."

During the summer of 1879, she made tentative plans to travel to Tennessee "to see the mountains and moonshiners that are to figure in my story." She had already chosen Rogersville, Tennessee, as her base of operations; for from there one "can make little excursions on horseback."[45] Although she had written Longfellow that she planned to leave Boston around August 25, no record has been discovered of her having visited in that area of Tennessee during the fall of 1879. Very possibly her plans were altered by the sudden decision of her husband, Edward McDowell, to visit Sherwood in Boston about that same time; for in the testimony Edward gave at Lilian's custody trial following Sherwood Bonner's death, he declared that he had "joined Kate in 1879 in Boston" and that "Lilian was here also." Since Sherwood had reported to Ruth in December, 1879, that Edward was working the Colorado mine fields, and since there is no evidence to place Edward in Boston earlier than the fall of 1879, it seems plausible to place his visit between August and December—the time between Sherwood's letter to Longfellow announcing her plans to go to Tennessee and her later letter to Ruth.

In the late fall of 1879, three more of Sherwood Bonner's stories appeared in the periodicals, to some of which she had gained entré only after the publication of *Like Unto Like*. In October, *Harper's Monthly* published a story based upon the yellow fever plague of Holly Springs, "The Revolution in the Life of Mr. Balingall"; in the October 18 issue of *Harper's Weekly*, the humorous and satirical "Maddy Gascar and the Professor" appeared; and in *Youth's Companion* for November 6 is "Lost and Found," a humorous story, renamed the "Finding of Absalom" in the *Suwanee River* collection.

In December, 1879, Sherwood Bonner wrote to Longfellow to advise him that she had submitted her recently completed long story to *Harper's Monthly;* but she felt that it was still not so accomplished and finished as she would have liked it to be.[46] She again thanked the poet for sending her the papers and periodicals she continued to receive from him. Later that same month, on Christmas Eve, Bonner again wrote Longfellow a brief note and enclosed a thank-you note from Lilian for the Christmas present Longfellow had sent her. This Christmas was the first and only one that Sherwood Bonner shared with her daughter in Boston.

Two months later, in February, 1880, Aunt Martha and Ruth McDowell and her husband arrived in New York City for a brief visit with Martha's brother;[47] and they were joined there by Sherwood and Lilian. On March 14, Sherwood wrote a chatty letter to Longfellow informing him of the family's New York activities and thanking him for having sent the tickets to "The Apollo Club" concert. Shortly thereafter Sherwood, Martha, and Lilian returned together to Boston; and Sherwood wrote to Longfellow on March 29 of her decision to sublet her Boston quarters, which had proved too small for the three of them, and to "board for a while before going to Penn Yan." She promised the poet that she would get to Cambridge at least once before leaving Boston, and little could Sherwood Bonner know that this visit would be her last with the poet who had long encouraged and befriended her.

During the next several months, Bonner's stories continued to find an outlet with a certain amount of regularity. In April, 1880, *Lippincott's* published one of Sherwood Bonner's most volatile stories, a story which resulted in numerous subscription cancellations by readers who objected to the miscegenation theme of "Volcanic Interlude." Two months later another of the Negro dialect stories, "Hieronymus Pop and the Baby," was published in *Harper's Monthly* (June, 1880). Bonner then took the step which, according to some, she had contemplated taking for the past five years.[48] She went to southern Illinois for the express purpose of establishing residence for the divorce action she now planned against Edward McDowell.[49] Sherwood Bonner spent the next fifteen months in Benton, DuQuoin County, Illinois, with a sister of Martha. While living here, she gathered the material for her Realistic stories with Illinois-prairie settings. This period was one of her most prolific, for she published during these fifteen months nine stories and a four-part serial that appeared in the fall of 1881 in *Lippincott's*. As was her custom whenever she was away from Boston for any appreciable length of time, Sherwood Bonner continued to write to Longfellow, although the letters were not so frequent as they had been in earlier years. Her primary interests continued to revolve around her fiction.

In the fall of 1880, three more stories appeared in the periodicals, all of them designed to appeal primarily to young people. In *Harper's Young People*, for the number of September 7, 1880, Sherwood Bonner produced a page of poems; this production was repeated for the issue of October 12, and in each case the work was richly illustrated. For the September issue of the *Wide Awake Pleasure Book*, Sherwood Bonner penned the amusing story of "Why Gran'mammy Didn't Like Pound Cake," a story designed to teach children a moral lesson about gluttony and deceit. And, finally, for the October 19, 1880, number of *Harper's Young People*, she wrote "The Angel in the Lilly Family."

Christmas of 1880 found Sherwood Bonner in better spirits than she had been for some time. She wrote to Longfellow that she had recently recovered from a long illness and that "she sees and seeks better days ahead." In the next six months, she published six additional stories, all of them with a Tennessee or Illinois setting, indicative of the fact that Bonner could handle well the dialect and characteristics of any area. On December 18, 1880, the humorous "Dr. Jex's Predicament" appeared in *Harper's Weekly;* the following month in the same magazine "Jack and the Mountain Pink" was printed. Less than two months later, and again in *Harper's Weekly*, appeared a Realistic story of treachery and deceit, "The Case of Eliza Bleylock." The following month, again suggestive of the influence of Longfellow upon Bonner's major work, *Harper's Monthly* published "Two Storms," the opening scene of which Longfellow himself had sketched in his own hand.[50] In the same month in which "Two Storms" was published, *Lippincott's* printed still another story of the Illinois prairie community, "Sister Weeden's Prayer." And, to complete this burst of creative energy, she published in *Harper's Weekly* in its May 28, 1881, number the Realistic "Lame Jerry."

In April, 1881, Sherwood's Aunt Martha had joined Lilian and Sherwood in Benton; and she remained with them until the final divorce decree was granted in an uncontested action. Martha then returned to Holly Springs with Lilian, and Sherwood Bonner went to St. Louis for a visit of about a month with Ruth and David McDowell.[51] When Sherwood returned to Holly Springs in July of that same summer, she wrote an extremely melancholy letter to Longfellow on August 7, 1881. She began with an apology for not having written "all this long time," and she explained that she had waited, hoping "to have something cheerful to tell you of my plans." She briefly alludes to the "terrible affair of the divorce" and to her long seige with pneumonia following the granting of the decree. She has now been in Holly Springs "for some time," attempting to settle her "great trouble about business affairs." David McDowell, Ruth's husband, wanted his wife's share of the Bonner estate in order to invest in a plantation in the "Mississippi Bottoms"; and he had offered to renounce all future claims to the Bonner property for the sum of fifteen hundred dollars. The alternative he offered was that the property be sold at public auction to satisfy his needs.

Sherwood explained to Longfellow that she did not want to sell the house because she, Lilian, and Martha needed a permanent home and because her only regular source of income was from farm rent. She also stated that her attorney had urged her to accept David's settlement figure and had insisted that he could obtain for her a long-term bank loan for the fifteen hundred dollars. Sherwood, however, was reluctant to undertake the obligation of a long-range mortgage on the house, partly because of her recent illness. She was, however, expecting "three hundred dollars in a week or so, from the Lippincott's," and she was working on a "Harper story that might fetch one hundred more."

She then proposed that Longfellow help her with the remainder so she could "die with dignity"; for she had recently detected a "*something*—I know not what—a hard lump or swelling—growing on my breast." She had immediately consulted a local doctor, who had advised her to "go East at once and see Dr. Hamilton or some prominent surgeon." She was evidently in some pain and saw no hope of future recovery: "It hurts—or burns—all the time." The melancholy letter concludes, rather pathetically, "Have I not long held my troubles from you? Love me a little for that. . . . Tell me if it is well with you and those you love—and let me soon hear from you—"[52]

Although Longfellow's reply to Sherwood Bonner has never been located, Professor Edward Wagenknecht suggests in *Longfellow: A Full-Length Portrait* that the poet did indeed promise to do what he could to help. Although he apparently promised to aid her after the middle of the following year, he died before he could redeem his pledge. His promise was honored by his daughter, Alice Longfellow; but the exact amount sent to Sherwood is not known. Sherwood

Bonner did write two letters of appreciation to Alice in 1882 to express her gratitude for all that Longfellow had done for her in life and for what Alice had done for her after his death.[53] Since "Bonner House" was inherited jointly by Martha and Lilian upon the death of Sherwood Bonner, it seems plausible that Sherwood had been able to work out a satisfactory arrangement with David McDowell without selling the house. Perhaps the three hundred dollars mentioned in Bonner's letter to Longfellow was for the four-part serial she wrote for *Lippincott's*, which appeared in the fall of 1881.

The serial was called "The Valcours," and again, as was the case with *Like Unto Like*, the setting is the Reconstruction Era. "The Valcours" was followed, though less rapidly than had been the case after the publication of *Like Unto Like*, with three more stories about the Illinois prairie. In the November 19, 1881, issue of *Harper's Weekly* appeared "The Barn Dance at the Apple Settlement." It was followed four months later by "Peacock Feathers," published in the same weekly on April 29, 1882. *Harper's Monthly* brought out one of the bitterest stories ever penned by Sherwood Bonner, "On the Nine Mile," in its May, 1882, number; and the last story published during the lifetime of Sherwood Bonner, "A Shorn Lamb," appeared in *Harper's Weekly* for August 26, 1882.

Despite the fact that in her August 7 letter to Longfellow Sherwood Bonner had implied the fear of an early death, not until the spring of 1882 did she firmly believe that she had less than a year to live.[54] It was then that she decided to return to Boston to busy herself with collecting her short stories for publication in book form. Shortly after settling in Boston, she became a close friend of Sophia Kirk, whose father was at that time an editor for *Lippincott's*.[55] One of her early biographers, B. M. Drake, suggests that Sophia Kirk was initially employed by Bonner as an amanuensis, for Sherwood was already beginning to tire easily, and at times to find writing itself a painful ordeal.[56] The only information as to the exact nature of the relationship between the two comes from Kirk herself. In the preface to *Suwanee River Tales*, she suggests that her friendship with Sherwood Bonner had been a recent one:

The stories which make up this collection have already appeared in various periodicals; they were revised and arranged in their present form in the summer of 1883, and before the close of that summer Sherwood Bonner had passed away. Now that the little book stands ready equipped to go before the public, it is deemed fitting that some words in memory of its author be prefixed to its pages. My sole qualification for writing them lies in the fact that it was my privilege to know Sherwood Bonner in the intimacy of a friendship which began late and ended, alas! too soon, but which was nevertheless a singularly close and complete one, and has helped to make even those parts of her life in which I had no share hardly less vivid to me than my own recollections.[57]

Apparently, Sherwood Bonner and Sophia Kirk had worked from the fall of 1882 through the spring of 1883 arranging the two volumes of short stories for publication. In the custody trial for Lilian following Bonner's death, Sophia Kirk testified that she had known Sherwood Bonner for the past two years and that, when Bonner had felt death drawing close and had returned to Holly Springs to die, Sophia Kirk had accompanied her and was with her at the moment of death. Sophia Kirk and Sherwood Bonner had returned on March 7, 1883, to Holly Springs; and Sherwood, who had then less than five months to live,[58] spent her time working on new material. Sophia Kirk testified at Lilian's trial that, at the time of her death, Sherwood Bonner had a book "very near completion" and that there were "notes in her own hand to complete." Kirk continued that Bonner also had another story completely finished, and "one more book which is to come on the market at Christmas time."[59] The short story referred to by Sophia Kirk was undoubtedly "Christmas Eve at Tuckyho," which appeared in *Lippincott's* in January, 1884, some six months after Sherwood Bonner's death; and the book due for Christmas publication was the collection of *Suwanee River Tales.* The novel alluded to, unfinished but very near to completion, was possibly *The Story of Margaret Kent*, published in 1886 by Henry Hayes, a pseudonym for Mrs. Ellen W. Olney Kirk, the sister-in-law of Sophia Kirk.

That Sherwood Bonner realized, during these months of enormous creative activity, that she would probably never recover from the cancer which attacked her at the age of thirty-four is indicated in one of the very few poems she published. On February 14, 1883, less than six months before her death, she composed "A Longed-For Valentine":

> Come to my aching heart, my weary soul,
> And give my thoughts once more their vanquished will:
> That I may strive and feel again the thrill

Of bounding hope, to reach its farthest goal.
Not Love, though sweet as that which Launcelot stole,
Nor Beauty, happy as a dancing rill,
Nor Gold, poured out from some fond miser's till,
Nor yet a name on Fame's immortal scroll—
But what I ask, O gracious Lord, from Thee,
If to Thy throne my piteous cry can reach,
When stricken down like tempest-riven tree,
Too low for prayer to wreak itself in speech,
Is but the fair gift—ah, will it e'er be mine?
My long lost Health for my dear Valentine.[60]

Although the details of the last eighteen months of Sherwood
Bonner's life are somewhat sketchy, she continued to work on her
fiction in Boston from the spring of 1882 until the spring of 1883 and
in Holly Springs during the last months of her life. Perhaps the best
single statement covering these last three months is found in Sophia
Kirk's account: "Concealing from all but one or two friends the
hopelessness of the prospect, she set herself bravely to work while it
was still light, and did work, with a persistence simply marvelous,
far into the shadows. . . . One July afternoon she began to dictate
some part of a story she was writing. A few sentences, uttered with
great difficulty, were transferred to the paper. Then she paused,
and a look which was unmistakable came over her face. Four days
later, July 22, 1883, she died.[61] She was buried in the Bonner lot in
Hill Crest Cemetery in Holly Springs in an unmarked grave in
accordance with her wishes.

CHAPTER 3

Dialect Tales

I *"Gentleman of Sarsar"*

O F the eleven stories that make up the collection *Dialect Tales* (1883), only two had not previously been published in periodical form: "The Gentlemen of Sarsar," the first story of the collection, and "Aunt Anniky's Teeth," a semiautobiographical sketch. The plot of "The Gentlemen of Sarsar" is extremely slight, as is usually the case with the local-color story. For want of something better to do, the protagonist, Mr. Ned Merewether, has come to Sarsar to collect a debt due his father from a certain Andy Rucker, the patriarch of the town, and a nineteenth-century version of William Faulkner's Flem Snopes. The town dupes the gullible Mr. Merewether into going on a fake manhunt, during which Merewether supposedly kills a Negro, Bud Kane, accidentally.

Almost immediately Bud Kane's wife, mother, mistress, pastor, and undertaker touch Merewether for conscience money, but they do so in such a way and in so convincing a manner that Merewether never suspects he is being taken. He feels fortunate in having escaped from the town with his life even without having collected the money due his father. The light does not dawn until about a week later when a Negro arrives at Merewether's home with a package from Andy Rucker, and Merewether is astonished to see the same Bud Kane whom he had supposedly killed:

"Bud Kane!"

"Yes, sir; dat's me. Mars Andy tole you I was dead; but dat wus jest a joke o' his. Somebody axed him what made him act so hateful to you, an' he said onct dar wus two men standin' on de Courthouse steps, an' one of 'em ups an' knocks de odder off de steps, an' dey had him up for 'salt an' battery. An' de Judge says, "What made you knock dat man offen de steps. He wus a stranger ter you, an' not a-doin' no harm." An' de man says, "I knows it, judge, I didn't have nothin' agin de fellow; but de truth is, *he stood so fair I couldn't help it.*"[1]

"The Gentlemen of Sarsar" displays many of the fine qualities that combined to make Sherwood Bonner a writer of much promise. Her adroit handling of Negro dialect is shown especially in the humorous expressions uttered by the young Negro boy who escorts Ned, Dee Jay; the object of the Negro chase, Bud Kane; and Bud's supposedly sorrowing mother, Mother Kane, who responds to Ned's expression of sorrow with the comment that "sorrow don't butter no corn-pone."[2] Local-color characteristics, as suggested by Professor Blankenship, are also abundant, such as the unexpected and incongruous comparisons, and the unusually perceptive commonsense expressions. Bonner also reveals her power of vivid description, notably in her sketch of the "gentlemen of Sarsar" mounted and dressed appropriately for the "niggar chase," which forms the basic plot of the story. Sherwood Bonner's strongest characteristic as a storyteller, however, is undoubtedly her humor, and "The Gentlemen" abounds in this quality.

The story is told from the first-person narrative point of view, and Bonner's treatment of the characters and incidents of the story is wholly credible. In this respect, she seems ahead of most local-color writers of the time who made their characters types rather than individuals. Bonner is able to distinguish among her short-story characters by changing dramatically the setting, the content, and the level-of-language from one story to the next. With the exception of the "Gran'mammy" stories, a reader of Bonner's fiction meets an enormous range of characters; they are from high and low society and from points as distant as the Mississippi Delta, the Southern Illinois plains, and the mountains of western Tennessee. Thus Bonner is able to suggest individuals rather than types; but, in the fiction of local-color writers such as Bret Harte, neither the locale nor the cast of characters changes. In such local colorists, there is always the murmuring pine, the quiet (or turbulent) stream, the cool gambler, the drunken cowboy, the prostitute with a heart of gold, and other repeated types. In Bonner's fiction, on the other hand, even stock characters take on an air of individuality because of the level of their language, the locale, or other distinguishing characteristics.

II *"On the Nine Mile"*

"On the Nine Mile," the second story of the collection, blends Realism with many of the characteristics of the local-color story. The setting is on the Southern Illinois prairie, and the point of view is again first person. Humor is initially the chief tone, and the reader has no reason to suspect that the story is anything but another of the endless local-color tales of the latter half of the century. The handling of dialect suggests that Bonner had an extremely sensitive ear for distinguishing among regional dialects. In this story Bonner adds to her usage of the Southwestern-humorist-school conventions by relying heavily on incongruous and unexpected comparisons—such as "Popperler women . . . got no more character than stale eggs"—garbled speech, and exaggerated type characters.

The element of Realism is timidly introduced in the manner of Hamlin Garland's *Main-Travelled Roads* with the allusion to the hard lot of the farmer. It is, however, the tragedy that befalls Janey Burridge, the protagonist, that emphasizes the stark Realism. The plot, at least for the first half of the story, can be concisely stated in a single sentence: Janey has been promised in marriage to Charley Winn, but shortly before the wedding she is thrown before a reaping machine and badly mangled: "Fur many a draggin' week poor Janey lay betwixt life an' death. The child wuz cut an' bruised over every part of her body. Two of her ribs wuz broke, an' one limb had been impaled on the guards of the sickle, an' wuz nearly sawed in two. That she should so much as survive the shock an' horrid wounds seemed a miracle; but the doctor brought her round at last, though he told her quite frank she would never be able ter walk again."[3]

That this tale is to be no sugarcoated love story is quickly indicated by Sherwood Bonner. Almost immediately Charley Winn visits the crippled Janey but not to offer her consolation. He begins by lamenting his own bad luck that has caused him to lose Janey:

"A-losin' me?" repeats Janey, very slow. "But I ain't dead, Charley, nor like ter die, the doctor says."

That hat went round in Charley's fingers as if it wuz possessed. "But you know, Janey," he stammered—"you know, a man hes to marry a woman ter do her shear o' the work. And you can't do anything."

Janey swallered a few times, an' then said, quite nateral, "Of course, Charley, you will be marryin' some one else before a great while?"

"Oh yes," he says. "My house is built you know, an' I've already got my seed in that fifty-acre lot. I shell have to git me a wife by next harvest-time, you know."[4]

In less than six months Charley does get himself a wife. The story does not end here, for the happy ending, in which a former alcoholic and Janey are married, somewhat mitigates the earlier Realistic tone of the story. In this regard, Bonner is close to Bret Harte, whose sentimentality ruined his Realism, and to the later Hamlin Garland, who also allowed Romantic attitudes to replace the harsh Realism, or Veritism, of his earlier stories. Bonner, then, in "On the Nine Mile" and in her other Southern Illinois stories, can be read as a transitional figure leaning toward a Realistic concept of fiction, but possessing at the same time a certain degree of Romanticism, especially in her story endings. One might recall in this connection her aversion to the ending of Henry James' *The American*, which she described to Longfellow as "wretched."

III   *"Hieronymus Pop and the Baby"*

The third story, "Hieronymus Pop and the Baby," is purely in the rich tradition of humorous Negro dialect stories. It first appeared in *Harper's Monthly*, and it was undoubtedly included in the collection of *Dialect Tales* because of the popularization of the Negro folktale at this time under the leadership of Joel Chandler Harris. The story itself is slight, but there is a strong element of satire in the plot in that the young boy Hieronymus gets into his difficulties because his family has gone to see a public hanging, and he has been elected to remain home with the youngest of the Pop brood: "He thought it a burning shame that he should not go to the hanging; but never had his mother been willing that he should have the least pleasure in life."

The baby cries incessantly, and Hieronymus finally decides the baby's plight is caused by the heat of the day. He therefore stuffs "poor little Tiddlekins into the well bucket, though it must be mentioned to his credit that he tied the baby securely in with his own suspenders," and then goes off with a friend to witness a dog fight. The family returns, discovers both Hieronymus and Tiddlekins missing, institutes a frantic search, and finally discovers the baby in the well. Tiddlekins is brought around with the aid of Judge Chamber's whiskey—a sponge bath for the baby and most of the quart to soothe Mr. Pop—and, when the baby sitter returns, he is led to the woodpile. Despite the slight plot and content, the story again reveals Bonner's capable handling of Negro dialect and characterization, and it illustrates the natural humor that pervades the majority of her stories.

IV *"Sister Weeden's Prayer"*

"Sister Weeden's Prayer" was first published in *Lippincott's* in April, 1881; and, as with "On the Nine Mile," the setting is again the Southern Illinois farm country. It is obvious that Sherwood Bonner was attempting in these stories to follow the literary practice of the local colorist in writing about the locale and the people best known and most familiar to the writer. Bonner's Illinois residence of fifteen months had given her sufficient opportunity to observe firsthand the people of the region and to depict them in the stories written during this period.

"Sister Weeden's Prayer" is both amusing and satiric: amusing because of the picturesque, exaggerated speech of its characters; and satiric because of the emphasis on the general lack of Christian charity among people and their willingness to condemn their neighbor without a hearing. The dialect used by Bonner to suggest the speech patterns of the inhabitants of Southern Illinois is indicative of Bonner's ability to distinguish among people of various regions as well as between people of different races:

> Yes, we had gethered at the river, as the song says, to get a sight as might have surprised the angels. It wuz four o'clock of a Sunday afternoon, an' they wuz all assembled to see young Roland Selph baptized by Preacher Powell, who expounded the Word four times a year at Big Muddy meetin'-house.
>
> It wuz a'most like a meracle. Roland wuz a hard case. My husband—who, bein' one o' the "swearin' Wallers," as they wuz called in Grandpar Waller's day, had a sort of ancesterl talent for usin' strong words—an' better that than for usin' strong drink, says I, when twitted, for what is words but a slap-dash thrown together of letters? an' if a man chooses 'em hard, like goose-quills, instead o' soft, like goose-down, an' nobody's hurt, then where's the harm?—well, my husband he allys said that Roland wuz the "darnedest man to cuss on the prairie." He never had had no bringin' up wuz the trouble. His father, a rele active, nice man, wuz killed in a mill six months before he wuz born, an' his mother she took on so that she didn't have no strength to git him even so far along as teethin'. So his grandmother she raised him on sheep's milk an' a peach-tree switch. Kicks an' cuffs wuz

sandwiched between the poor child's meals, until the old woman died an' left him, kithless an' kinless in the land. A wild'lookin' lad he wuz, with a shock o' black hair that you couldn't 'a combed with a wool-card, an' big eyes bold as the hub of a wheel, an' clothed summer an' winter in rags! He wuz mightily in demand at harvest-time, for he wuz as strong as a horse, an' hadn't had a chill since his grandmother broke 'em on his at the age of fourteen with black pepper an' molasses an' santonine, an' a bag o' camphor at the pit of his stomach.[5]

The satire is directed broadly against those who delight in casting the first stone. One of the ladies of the Baptist Society, Sister Biscoe, has been observed sewing on the Lord's Day; as a result, her fellow sisters agree that they "must expel Dorothy Biscoe from the society an' leave her to the mercy of God." Surely there is an element of satirization intended by Bonner which is directed at the "holier-than-thou" attitude of such religious hypocrites, but the satire is somewhat alleviated by the forgiveness freely expressed by all when they learn the circumstances of Sister Biscoe's servile work on the Sabbath. It turns out that Sister Biscoe and her two daughters had agreed to make a Baptismal suit for Roland:

"The long and the short of it is that I soon saw Roland wuz a-tremblin' between two worlds. He wuz that unregenerate that he wouldn't face the public at Big Muddy without the befittin' clothes, yet the Spirit wuz so workin' within him that he had set his heart on sealin' himself to God the comin' Sunday. I thought of suggestin' to him to wait until Brother Powell came round again, but, seein' as how he wuz just out of the devil's clutches by a needle's length, as you may say, I didn't dare to say 'put it off' to him."[6]

Sherwood Bonner was a religious person who at the same time did not consider formal worship necessarily indicative of strong moral character. Like Emily Dickinson, she could keep the Sabbath while staying at home; and she manages in "Sister Weeden's Prayer" to rebuke, although gently, those who flaunt their assumed piety.

V "Aunt Anniky's Teeth"

"Aunt Anniky's Teeth" is one of the Negro dialect stories that belongs to the group of "Gran'mammy" stories, despite the fact that Gran'mammy does not actually play a role in this tale. The story apparently had some basis in fact, for Sherwood Bonner portrays her mother, her father, her sister, and herself in this narrative. The story is told from the same point of view as are the "Gran'mammy" tales, that of the first-person narrator. As the title suggests, the loosely organized plot has to do with a set of false teeth that Dr. Charles Bonner ("Mars' Charles," as Aunt Anniky calls him, for "she had been one of our old servants, and always called my father Mars' Charles") has had made for her in return for her devoted nursing of Mrs. Bonner through a recent illness. Mr. Bonner had told Aunt Anniky that he would buy her anything she wanted; and, in the typical humorous dialect of the Negro, Aunt Anniky requests a set of teeth:

"Well, Mars' Charles, . . . to tell you de livin' trufe, my soul an' body is a-yearnin' fur a han'-sum chany set o' teef."
"A set of teeth!" cried father, surprised enough. "And have you none left of your own?"
"I has gummed it fur a good many ye'rs," said Aunt Anniky, with a sigh; "but not wishin' ter be ongrateful ter my obligations, I owns ter havin' five nateral teef. But dey is po' sogers: dey shirks battle. One ob dem's got a little somethin' in it as lively as a speared worm, an' I tell you when anything teches it, hot or cold, it jest makes me *dance!* An' anudder is in my top jaw, an' ain't got no match fur it in de bottom one; an' one is broke off nearly to de root; an' de las' two is so yaller dat I's ashamed to show 'em in company, an' so I lif's my turkey tail ter my mouf every time I laughs or speaks."[7]

Dr. Bonner arranges for the teeth, but their acquisition by Aunt Anniky proves to be only the beginning of her story. One night she is called to nurse an old Negro named Uncle Ned; and, as he tells the story, Aunt Anniky's teeth quite literally disintegrate:

"Well, it war de fift' night o' de fever," said Uncle Ned, "an' I wuz a-tossin' an' a-moanin' an' ole Anniky jes lay back in her cheer an' snored as ef a dozen frogs wuz in her throat. I wuz a-perishin' an' a-burnin—wid thirst— an' I hollered to Anniky; but lor! I might as well 'a hollered to a tombstone! It wuz ice I wanted; an' I knowed dar wuz a glass somewhar on my table wid cracked ice in it. Lor! lor! how dry I wuz! I neber longed fur whiskey in my born days ez I panted fur dat ice. It wuz powerful dark, fur de grease wuz low in de lamp, an' de wick spluttered wid a dyin' flame. But I felt aroun', feeble like an' slow, till my fingers touched a glass. I pulled it to me, an' I run my han' in an' grabbed de ice, as I s'posed, an' flung it in my mouf, an' crunched and' crunched— . . . *It wuz Anniky's teef.*"[8]

The upshot of the unfortunate destruction of Anniky's teeth is that she and Ned agree to marry "to unite their interests," as Dr. Bonner

expresses it; and for a wedding gift Dr. Bonner presents Aunt Anniky with a new set of teeth. The plot scarcely seems worth the
summary, but the story remains, nevertheless, a significant one in
view of the time of its publication. Its inclusion in *Dialect Tales*
suggests that, although Sherwood Bonner was now concentrating on
semi-Realistic tales, she had not completely abandoned her interest
in the Negro dialect narrative with which she had won her initial
success. Again, the story abounds with the characteristics of the
Southwest humorists, as is evidenced by the dialect reproduced
above, by the presence of the typical Negro character, and by the
humorous effect of such incongruous comparisons as "Uncle Ned
tottered on his legs like an unscrewed fruit stand," as well as by the
overall humorous appeal of the story's plot.

VI *"Dr. Jex's Predicament"*

"Dr. Jex's Predicament," originally published in *Harper's Weekly*
on December 18, 1880, when Sherwood Bonner was living in Perry
County in Southern Illinois, is set in Kentucky; but it could hardly
be called one of her Realistic stories of frontier life. The sketch is
carried primarily by the Negro, this time called Uncle Brimmer,
who "walked all the way from Mississippi to Kentucky, with his
things tied up in a meal sack, and presented himself before Mabel,
announcing affably that he had come to 'stay on.' " The plot is built
around a house call made by the country doctor, Dr. Jex, to see
Uncle Brimmer during an illness, and around the difficulties the
good-natured but elderly doctor undergoes in an attempt to get into
Uncle Brimmer's loft-room. The sketch has little to recommend it
beyond the humorous appeal of the slight plot. There is little dialect
in it, and no carefully drawn characters.

VII *"In Aunt Mely's Cabin"*

The next of the *Dialect Tales*, "In Aunt Mely's Cabin," was published in *Lippincott's* in February, 1878. In it, Sherwood Bonner
seems at the halfway mark between local color and Realism, for the
plot depends on mistaken identity. The story is told from the third
person, or objective, point of view; and the chief focal point of the
early part of the narrative is descriptive—a successful attempt to
evoke a mood of loneliness and impending doom. The time is midnight, the night is "starless," and "the sky [bends] so close to earth
that one might fancy the very steam of the world's passions con-

densed in the black clouds that rolled heavily across it: no sound save the ceaseless, soft plashing of the Mississippi waves." Decay is everywhere evident, from the "fluttering rags that hung from a dingy tenement-house" to "a flat level, where new workshops, ruins of burnt houses, and long cotten-sheds were crowded together."

Even the sun "rose gloomily" the next morning, and the silver moonlight "that had been almost poetic the night before" now yields to the harsh rays of the morning sun which reveal the town's "squalid ugliness. The street near the river, once a fine and fashionable promenade, now seemed built of the very skeletons of houses, so busily had decay been at work, and so little had been done to stop its advances." The time is that of the Mardi Gras season, several years after the Civil War; and the story is set some miles above New Orleans where the Mississippi River divides the states of Louisiana and Mississippi.

The central character is a fugitive, a young man fresh from a crime in his own city, Hopefield, which lies just across the river. The description of the protagonist, Phil Vickers, emphasizes the decay and hopelessness evident everywhere in the South after the Civil War; "The face was one common enough in a malarious country—a yellow, lean, sharp face; besides this, it was a young, weak, passionate face. The sunbeams were kind and did not wake him. The eyelids pressed close upon the eyes, and the lashes lay motionless on the thin cheeks."[9] Nevertheless, the point is made and reiterated that Vickers had never served in the war, and it is implied that he had been too young for military service. Bonner suggests that those frequently most crippled by the war and its aftermath were those who played no role in it; they are accidental victims of their physical environment, or of fate; and, with this concept, Bonner actually anticipates the early Naturalism of Stephen Crane, Theodore Dreiser, and Frank Norris.

Vickers, realizing that he will be pursued, seeks safety in the Negro quarter at the home of Aunt Mely, a former slave whom he had known in earlier and better days. The description of Aunt Mely's cabin also emphasizes the run-down condition of the South itself and the devastation wrought by war: "Aunt Mely's house was poised on the side of the bluff like a rocking-stone. Back of it was a struggling garden, protected from the goats by a queer sort of fence made of all the refuse stuff Aunt Mely could find—broad planks and narrow planks, old fence rails, sticks of wood and brush-heaps. Of the house itself you could not say that one part was worse than another. It seemed to hang together by attenuated threads. Samson in his days of bibs and long-gowns could have brought it about his ears with a vigorous infantine kick."[10]

From this point on, however, the story, Realistic and almost Naturalistic in its promising beginning, is rendered largely ineffectual because a Romantic view of life is injected. The former slave agrees to hide Vickers, the "posse" of three arrive at Aunt Mely's cabin, and Vickers is confronted by Tom Jack, the very man whose murder he is fleeing. In an ending suggestive of O. Henry, it is brought out that Vickers, seeing his wife embrace another man in his cabin, had fired and fled. His wife's "lover" was Tom Jack's sister who had dressed in her brother's suit for the Mardi Gras ball. Vickers' wife then arrives with the news that the girl will recover; and the brother, Tom Jack, yields to Vickers' wife's request that he make his peace with her husband. The reader is left, therefore, with the conventional and trite "all's well that ends well" conclusion.

Despite its obvious weaknesses, the story clearly reveals the transitional state of American literature and the fiction of Sherwood Bonner: both are caught between Realism and Romanticism. In the final analysis, the story barely deserves the designation of local color, and yet one can discover the tendency toward Realism in the opening description of the misery, poverty, loneliness, and squalor of the environment in which the principal character moves. Had the story been written five years earlier, Aunt Mely's dialect and humor would undoubtedly have been emphasized, as they were in the Gran'mammy stories. If the story had been written five years later, the snap-of-the-whip ending and the implausible stream of coincidences would very likely have given way to dark and bitter truth. Instead, the last view we have of Betty and Phil Vickers is one of tender regard and mutual love: "But Little Betty drew the tired head to her tender heart and looked defiantly round the others, as if throwing all the splendor of her faithful love between Phil and any look of contempt or blame."[11]

VIII   *"The Case of Eliza Bleylock"*

The next of the *Dialect Tales*, which was also written during Bonner's residence in Illinois, was initially published in *Harper's Weekly* on March 5, 1881. The setting is the mountain region of Tennessee; and, although the credibility of part of the story is strained, Bonner at last forsakes the conventional ending and tells a story of deceit and death. The title, "The Case of Eliza Bleylock," seems at first ill-chosen; for the story revolves initially around Eliza's sister, Jenny, and her fiancé, Dick Oscar. The chief occupation of the Bleylock family and of most of the Cumberland characters is moonshining. The local revenue officer plants a peddler, Marcus Pond, in the Bleylock residence in order to learn the location of the still.

Pond, however, is unsuccessful in his attempts to pry the information from Eliza; but Jenny, her pride momentarily hurt by Oscar's seeming rejection of her love, leads Pond to the still. The peddler informs the revenue officer, Captain Peters, and the very next day the Bleylocks and Oscar are surprised at the still and taken into custody. The assumption is that Eliza has supplied the information to the peddler since she had been the object of his courtship, and her protests to the contrary are ignored. Oscar and Jenny eventually marry; and Jenny, afraid of what Oscar might do if he should ever discover that she, not Eliza, betrayed him, keeps silent. As for Eliza,

She repeated her denial of having been a traitor, but no one ever believed her. She worked hard, and was used roughly. She had never been strong. Sometimes she stole away and nursed Jenn's baby, that seemed to love her; but never when Dick Oscar was at home.

One day, sitting by the spring alone, too weak since a long while to work, she leaned her head against a tree, . . . [and] she died. . . . And she was buried, with very little said about it, in the valley.[12]

Admittedly, the plot is slight, and the characters are not too finely drawn; nevertheless, the story shows a marked departure for Bonner away from the folk humor of her early stories and toward the accurate depiction of people at their worst as well as at their best in the true manner of the budding Realists.

IX   *"The Barn Dance at the Apple Settlement"* and *"Lame Jerry"*

The ninth story in this collection is wholly a narrative of reminiscence, for Sherwood Bonner recalls a visit she made to her sister's home in Tennessee. The story, "The Barn Dance at the Apple Settlement," is told from the first-person point of view; and it adds nothing either to the knowledge of Bonner's life or to her status as a professional writer. The next story, however, "Lame Jerry," is a successor to "The Case of Eliza Bleylock"; for some of the same characters are present, notably Jane and Dick Oscar. The protagonist is Lame Jerry, who as the story opens has been grievously assaulted for having informed on some mountaineer moonshiners. He is slowly nursed back to health by Jane, who, as Dick continually reminds her, has "got a soft spot in yo' heart fur sneaks, on account o' yo' sister." During Jerry's absence from home, his only daughter, Cordy, thinking her father dead, leaves with another moonshiner named Discoe.

The narrative then becomes a story of revenge and finally one of frustrated revenge. Lame Jerry stalks Discoe, waiting for the right opportunity to kill him for having led his daughter into a sinful life: "The day came at last. Discoe was cleaning his gun in the woods, unarmed, inert, unsuspicious. Behind him, huge and misshapen, the hunchback crawled and coiled and sprung. There was little resistance—the surprise was too complete—and Lame Jerry's arm was nerved by hate and madness. When Discoe was dead the murderer dragged his body to Caney Fork, and weighting it with rocks, saw it sink beneath the hiding waters. Then he went to his daughter."[13]

Cordy, thinking Discoe will return, refuses to go home with her father, as he suggests when he visits her the next day. Lame Jerry, confident that his daughter will not wait forever for a man he knows can never return, is willing enough to wait. It soon becomes apparent to the father that Cordy is pregnant and that she feels she cannot leave without her husband. The conclusion finds Cordy and her baby dead in childbirth, "And Lame Jerry was left to live with his money—and his memories."

The particular aspect of both "Eliza Bleylock" and "Lame Jerry" that makes them Realistic rather than Romantic is that there is no regeneration on the part of the sinner, no redemption—Lame Jerry is left to taste fully the bitter results of his sinful, immoral, or unfeeling ways. The stories of the 1880s surely reveal a different emphasis and a differing view of life than did Bonner's earlier, largely humorous, local-color tales.

X *"Jack and the Mountain-Pink"*

The last story of the collection, "Jack and the Mountain-Pink," which first appeared in January 29, 1881, in *Harper's Weekly*, has its setting in the Cumberland Mountain region of Tennessee, not far from Nashville, in the summer of 1878. Although many of the same characters from other stories of this region appear, the primary emphasis of "Mountain-Pink" is on humor. The characters presented are typical of the local-color story as conceived by such writers as Bret Harte and George W. Harris: the principal type characters of the region are present in the depiction of the typical moonshiner (Jack Boddy), the ludicrous revenue officer who is repeatedly fooled by the moonshiners (Jim Peters), the widow (Widow Hicks) with her marriageable and barefoot daughter (Sincerity Hicks), and the neutral observer from Nashville (young Selden). The story is told from the third-person point of view; the slight plot consists of the arrest and escape of Jack Boddy; and the total effect is merely humorous. The story reveals again the very essence of Bonner's ability—her fine ear for dialect—and it additionally emphasizes her familiarity with the traditions of the Southwest humorist and of the local-color literary movements.

Of the eleven stories that constitute *Dialect Tales*, three are carryovers from the Negro dialect type that comprise the bulk of Bonner's first literary efforts and are written primarily to entertain in the tradition of the oral tale. Five of the others are written about life in the Tennessee-Kentucky mountain area, and two of these are in the vanguard of Realistic literature because of their emphasis on exposing the weaknesses of man's base nature. Two others of the collection are set on the Southern Illinois prairie; in these, the emphasis is also on the realities of life as it was lived; and the details suggest the hard lot of the farmers and the weary lives of their women. The other school represented by a single story is the local-color movement, although several of the Realistic tales also possess characteristics of local color.

In summary, the *Dialect Tales* reveal a shifting of subject matter and a developing attitude toward life which in itself is a characteristic of Realism and Naturalism. Undoubtedly, the literary environment of Boston and the increasingly pointed Realism of William Dean Howells and Henry James, with whose work Bonner was familiar, combined to make Bonner more keenly aware than most of her fellow local colorists of the emergence in American literature of a new kind of fiction—the substitution of Realism for Romance.

CHAPTER 4

Suwanee River Tales

S HERWOOD Bonner's only other collection of short stories was not published until after her death. Entitled *Suwanee River Tales*, the narratives are of more biographical than literary interest. The fact, however, that these stories constituted Sherwood Bonner's training ground makes their examination imperative. Unlike the stories collected in *Dialect Tales*, those of *Suwanee River* are grouped according to subject matter in three divisions. The first section, entitled simply "Gran'mammy," contains six tales that are mostly about Bonner's childhood in Holly Springs. The four stories of the second group, which are collectively called "Four Sweet Girls of Dixie," are essentially autobiographical stories set in the Civil War and Reconstruction Era. The title of the third group, consisting of eight stories, suggests the subject matter and the appeal of all of these: "A Ring of Tales for Younger Folks."

I "Gran'mammy"

The first selection in the "Gran'mammy" grouping, "Gran'-mammy," merely introduces the character of Gran'mammy, the old Negro nurse whom Sherwood Bonner "loved and mourned as an old friend."[1] She was called "Gran'mammy rather than the conventional "Mammy" because she had reared Bonner's mother, Mary Wilson Bonner, as well as Sherwood. In this sketch, numerous references occur to Sherwood, to her sister Ruth, and to the mother, "Miss Mary." The principal characteristic of this and all other Gran'mammy tales is Bonner's adept and skillful handling of Negro dialect. Three years before Joel Chandler Harris published his first Uncle Remus story entitled "Negro Folklore. The Story of Mr. Rabbit and Mr. Fox, as Told by Uncle Remus" (The *Constitution*, July 20, 1879), Sherwood Bonner wrote ". . . the first negro dialect stories published in a Northern journal."[2] As one of Bonner's

earlier biographers has written, "The "Gran'mammy Stories" reveal
with force and beauty the characteristics of the old Southern
'mammy,' who deserves a modest place with 'The chaste and sage
Dame Euryclei' and fair Juliet's nurse; and Sherwood Bonner has
made posterity her debtor by preserving the lineaments of this
picturesque personage whose place formerly was of so much consequence in the Southern home."[3]

Eight years after the appearance of the first of the Gran'mammy
tales, Mark Twain expressed great pride in his own handling of
dialect in his famous "Explanatory," which preceded the contents of
Huckleberry Finn:

In this book a number of dialects are used, to wit: the Missouri negro
dialect; the extremist form of the backwoods Southwestern dialect; the
ordinary "Pike County" dialect; and four modified varieties of this last. The
shadings have not been done in a haphazard fashion, or by guesswork; but
painstakingly, and with the trustworthy guidance and support of personal
familiarity with these several forms of speech. I make this explanation for
the reason that without it many readers would suppose that all these characters were trying to talk alike and not succeeding. THE AUTHOR[4]

But in the early to the mid-1870s, Bonner was delighting readers of
the *Youth's Companion* and *Lippincott's* with the picturesque
speech and imagery of her real as well as fictional Gran'mammy:

"I never seed sich chillern in all my born days," she cried one day, when
Ruth interrupted her in the midst of custard-making, to beg leave to get
into the kettle of boiling soap that she might be clean once for all, and never
need another bath; while Sam, on the other side, entreated that she would
make three "points" of gravy with the fried chicken for dinner. (Sam always
came out strong on pronunciation; his very errors leaned to virtue's side.)
"I clar to gracious," said poor gran'mammy, "you'll drive all de sense
clean outen my head. How Miss Mary 'xpec's me ter git a dinner fitten fur
white folks ter eat, wid you little onruly sinners furever under foot, is mo'
dan I kin say. An' here's Leah an' Rachel, my own gran'chillern, a no mo'
use ter me dan two tarbabies!"[5]

The initial story in *Suwanee River Tales* is one that Gran'mammy
had told to Sherwood when she was about twelve years old; and she
describes it as a story "so complete, so naive, so crowded with
moral, as to deserve a chapter all to itself."[6] In "Why Gran'mammy
Didn't Like Pound-Cake," Bonner tells the reader that her

Gran'mammy had been too ill to attend a recent birthday party in the Bonner household; therefore, Ruth and Catherine had "piled up a basket with good things and started off, swinging it on a long pole, of which Ruth held one end and I the other."[7] When the three children had arrived at Gran'mammy's cabin—for Sam, the girls' younger brother, had accompanied Kate and Ruth—Gran'mammy had immediately spied the slice of cake in the basket and had begun to narrate to her visitors the story of why she neither eats nor likes "de poun'-cake." When Gran'mammy had been about as old as Kate, she had been given a pound cake to take to her mother; and, instead, she had eaten it herself and had been affected with the inevitable stomach aches and cramps in the middle of the night.

In this story, a very slight one, the moral is aimed directly at the listening children: "many a good thing is turned ter poison if you take it on de sly. You's mighty safe ter pend on dat ar trufe!"[8] The genius of Bonner in handling Negro dialect in the tradition of the local colorists is obvious, but what may not be so obvious is her knowledge of the conventions of the Southwestern humorist school. In the following passage, also taken from Bonner's introduction to "Gran'mammy," one can recognize many such characteristics, found also in the work of Josh Billings, Artemus Ward and Mark Twain, whose writings were influenced by the Southwest Humor school. The use of dialect is apparent, as are the garbled spellings, gross exaggerations ("Arter about a million years of sufferin' . . . "), incongruous comparisons, and far-fetched or elaborate similes:

"Ter be short wid it, chillern, I listened ter de v'ice, an' when I got home, I handed de slice o' weddin'-cake to ole Mis', an' tole her all about de weddin', looking as innercent as a lily; an' all de time was dat poun'-cake hid away under de waggin seat.

"Jes as soon as night fell, I stole up de stairs to ole Mis's room, an' I snuggled under de bed, an' i *et de poun'-cake!* De fust bite tasted as if all de stars had turned to cake an' was a-meltin' in my mouth; but to tell you de trufe,—, Sam, you listen,—I had ter sort of' *push de las'* piece down.

"Arter about a million years o' sufferin', de doctor gat dar; . . . an' de nex' mornin' dar I was, gaspin' like a fish out o' water, but saved!"[9]

Gran'mammy's second tale, "The Night the Stars Fells," is based upon the famous meteoric shower of 1833. The story illustrates no particular theme or moral, unless it is that the grace of God cares for all living things; for, toward the end of the story, Sherwood Bonner's

mother, then a small child of four, is suddenly missed. After a long
search, she is found sound asleep at the top of a well shaft; and her
mother is heard by Gran'mammy to say that "He hath given His
angels charge over her to keep her in all her ways." The principal
appeal and merit of the story again lies in both the Realistic dialect
and the intense power of description exhibited, a description made
even more telling by its rendition in the Negro dialect: "Jes' think,
my chillern, of all de bright stars above you shootin' down, down
from de heavens! De whole air filled wid 'em, like a shirl o' flyin'
goose feathers shaken out of a bag." This description is followed by
an even more awful display: "Den dar wus balls of fire, not fallin',
but dartin' through half circles, till they bust into million o' red
sparkles, or went out on a sudden, leavin' behind 'em long trails, jes'
like a comet's tail, on'y wilder an' redder."

"Some o' dese balls would stay quite still, like God's great fiery eyes
lookin' on a sinful world. An' dar wus lines o' pale yaller light,—God's
writin' on de walls o' heaven—driftin' along as de wind would blow. Sometimes dey would wriggle like snakes o' fire, an' agin dey would draw demselves up like livin' things, till dey wus nothin' but a small cloudy blaze. An'
over de whole earth dar wus a shinin' light, such as I've seen at twilight
arter a blazin' sunset, on'y more beautiful,—like de glory roun' de throne o'
God, I've thought sence.

"But what wid de howlin' an' de screechin' o' de darkies aroun' me, it
seemed as if I mus' lose my senses. Dar wus as many as seventy-five
niggers,—an' every man, an' woman, an' chile among 'em wus crazy wid
fear.

"Dey had rushed from der beds,—some wid quilts or blankets thrown
aroun' them, some shiverin' in der night-close,—and chillern, if you believe
me, some o' dem niggers had torn off every rag o' clothin' dat dey had on,
an' wus crouchin' hard on de groun', as if dey wus tryin' to force a way into
de bowels o' de earth, to hide demselves from dat sarchin' light.

"Some wus prayin', some shoutin' out der sins. Alsy Herdon—a little slim
yaller gal dat none of us never had no suspicions on—came runnin' to me,
her teeth all chatterin', aholdin' out my best head-handkercher, dat I had
missed mor'n a month back.

" 'I stole it! I stole it!' she screamed. 'Take it quick, Molly Wilson! O Lord
God, forgive my sins!' An' down she fell, all twistin' an' writhin' an' foamin'
at de mouth.

"Oh, it was a dreadful time! An' yit, chillern, in de midst of it, I couldn't
help laughin' at an ole fool of a rooster dat hopped up on de fence as lively as
a spring chicken, an' begun to crow, thinkin' mornin' had come an' found
him nappin'.' "[10]

While the above passages cast little additional light on "Gran'mammy," they do reveal Bonner's powers of invention and description, as well as her power of recall; for the scenes she describes so vividly had taken place some sixteen years before her birth and were therefore described by "Gran'mammy" at least twenty-five or thirty years after their occurrence.

The unusual common sense and understanding of "Gran'mammy" is shown in the next tale, "How Gran'mammy Broke the News." The title is slightly deceptive, for the news is good, not bad. Kate Bonner's cousin, Allan Edmundson, had earlier been reported killed in battle during the Civil War. The family was still in mourning; and Aunt Sarah, Allan's mother, was then living with the Bonner's, having been burned out of her own home. Bonner describes the homecoming in overly sentimental terms, but the role played by "Gran'mammy" is the high point of the story:

There was a hawthorne hedge around the place, and looking through its interstices I saw a soldier in grey coming toward our gate. The sun was in my eyes, and the first thing I noticed about him was that he was extremely ragged. Then I saw that he had a long tawny beard, the like of which I had never seen before.

As he drew nearer, his face seemed familiar; those honest blue eyes—what! did my own eyes deceive me? Could it be?

"O God of all mercies!" breathed, rather than spoke, dear gran'mammy, sinking to her knees, and stretching out her arms to the coming figure.[11]

Kate, with her childish enthusiasm, had wanted to rush home to break the good news to Aunt Sarah; but the wise old black "Mammy" knew better:

"O Allan! do not waste another minute. Come quickly to poor Aunt Sarah!"

But gran'mammy laid a hand on Allan's arm.

"Stop, honey, stop; Miss Katie you forgit. Don't you know dat joy itse'f is sometimes more dan a breakin' heart kin bear? Mis' Sarah is mighty frail; an' she mus' be made ready to meet dis shock, for dis is jes' as much a shock as de lie dat struck her down. Blessed be de Lord for sendin' de last so quick on de heels of de fust. Now, Miss Katie, you jes' take Mars' Allan in de house, an' tell your ma to give him some coffee an' hoe-cake right away ter put a little color in his po' cheeks, an' I'll go up stairs, an' break de news ter Mis' Sarah. Now, whatever you do, Mars' Allan, don't come up till I say de words."[12]

Whether or not "Gran'mammy" was correct about slowly and gently breaking the news one can never know, but the Bonner family thought her much the wiser for her method:

> "Mother feared it would be too much for her; but, thanks perhaps to our dear old happy gran'mammy, Aut Sarah had been gently led to her heaven-like joy. In a little while she was lying on the sofa, her hand clasping Allan's, her face radiant as an angel's, while we all gathered round to listen to our soldier-boy. He did not say a great deal; he was not strong enough yet. But his face wore an expression of peace it was pleasant to see. He watched our pretty guest with the most unabashed eagerness, yet with so much reverence in his gaze that the veriest coquette must have been touched. Poor fellow! his eyes were beauty-starved, and they feasted now, even as his heart feasted on the love we gave him in such rich store.
>
> And as to feasting of still another kind—well we all promised never to tell how much our hungry soldier managed to stow away under his grey jacket; but gran'mammy, quite her comfortable fat self again, said with a chuckle:—
>
> "Mighty lucky dar wus gwine ter be a party in de house. Dunno how else Mars' Allan would 'a' got enough ter eat."[13]

One of the most amusing narratives about Gran'mammy concerns the superstitions of the American Negro at a particular time in history. In this tale, "Coming Home To Roost," which takes place immediately after Lee's surrender, the Negroes of Holly Springs assemble "to celebrate their freedom by a grand colored camp-meeting on Cold Water Creek."[14] Aunt Becky Bonner, Gran'mammy's daughter and the Bonner family's laundress, attends the meeting; and, while there, she imagines herself to be "tricked," or bewitched. She comes home to die, and the efforts of three physicians, including those of Dr. Charles Bonner, fail to convince her that she is not about to die. Finally, Kate's cousin Henry, a medical student, takes Aunt Becky under his care; and he saves her by pretending to believe her story about being "tricked" and by casting counter spells to drive out "the snakes and demons" that have entered Aunt Becky's body.

The story is interesting both for its humor—since Bonner is ever mindful of the humorous possibilities when she writes of the superstitions of the Bonner Blacks—and for its insight into the customs and beliefs concerning the African heritage of the nineteenth-century Negroes. In response to Cousin Henry's question, "What is a Hoodoo witch?" Dr. Charles Bonner replied as follows:

"The priest of the Hoodoo religion, I suppose," said my father; "at least, some one who has the inside track of things."

"There is really then a Hoodoo religion?"

"Oh, yes,—though I don't know its tenets; and I'm sure I don't wish to! Only the most ignorant negroes believe in it; yet, strange to say, the most devout Christians among them stand in mortal terror of these priests, and will even attend their repulsive rites and ceremonies, in the fear of being tricked should they turn the cold shoulder."

"How do they manage this tricking business?"

"The most common way is to hide a fetich under the victim's door-step or in his bed."

"What sort of a fetich?" said Henry, who seemed to be fast developing into a little crooked thing that asks questions.

"Either a little wooden image of God, or a small ball of bedevilment, made up of feathers, rope-ends, locks of hair, dead insects, and other objects too disgusting to mention. With these, and the fine spell of an 'evil eye' the sorcerers seem to work their sweet will with the negroes who displease them."[15]

The incident recalls Mark Twain's treatment in *Huckleberry Finn* of Jim's hair-ball, which Jim "used to do magic with." The scene in which Cousin Henry cures Becky is well staged by Bonner, and it bears some retelling. Always attentive to detail, Bonner recreates the setting with considerable care:

"The back-yard was densely packed with negroes, but not one was allowed to enter. Inside the cabin, the scene was worthy of a painter. The primitive lamp—an iron bowl of lard-oil, with a wick floating on the surface—burned with a black smoke above the flame, and cast strange, flaring, hobgoblin shadows on the white-washed walls. Henry drew a chalk circle in the middle of the floor, marking inside of it ridiculous designs, which it pleased him to call cabalistic. Then he swung a lighted censer, chanted a Latin hymn, and was withal so grave that even I dared no longer smile, though the pungent odor of the incense set me sneezing!

Gran'mammy bared her daughter's swollen rheumatic limbs, and Henry rubbed them gently for about half an hour. Then he said: "I find, Aunt Beckey, that the snakes are now all in the right leg. The fetich has troubled them so much that they are trying to get out. The only thing to do is cut open the foot, and they will drop out of themselves. Are you willing?"

"Go on," said Aunt Beckey.

"Stand back, all of you!" said Henry. "No one must come near me but Sam. He must hold the basin."

I saw a twinkle in the small boy's eye, and I crept pretty near myself, unrebuked by my absorbed cousin. He pierced the foot with a sharp lancet, and the blood flowed freely. The light was so dim that for all my efforts I could not quite see what was going on. But I noticed that Sam held the oblong box in one hand; and from time to time, an exclamation from one of this precious pair,—"There is another!" "Don't let it get away!" "Four, is it?" or some such significant cry,—set us all quivering with excitement.

"That is all," said Henry at last. "She is saved."

He bound up the foot, and took the bandage from Aunt Beckey's eyes. "Fetch another light," he said quietly.

Then he held the basin, so that she could examine its contents; and there were at least six wicked-looking little snakes. "Those who have eyes to see, let them see," said that wretched Henry, without so much as the flicker of an eyelash!

I can hear Aunt Beckey's scream of joy to this day! Then how she wept! What blessings she called down on the head of the arch impostor! What shouts of "Glory! Glory!" resounded through the little room! How the darkies outside took up the strain, and all night long praised the Lord in singing and in prayer."[16]

Apart from the humorous appeal and the historical footnote, the story again emphasizes Bonner's ability to depict accurately incidents and scenes common to mid-nineteenth-century American folkways.

The last of the "Gran'mammy" stories is about the death of Gran'mammy; and, although the story is most assuredly a sentimental one, Bonner's descriptive ability is everywhere evident, from the description of the day itself to that of the last gifts that Gran'mammy bestows upon her loved ones, her "white chillern," Sherwood and Ruth Bonner. Appropriately entitled "Gran'mammy's Last Gifts," this story is tenderly told. As Sherwood Bonner describes the setting and the gifts themselves—two gold coins to Sam, ". . . to buy a nice fat turkey every Sunday as long as de money holds out"; her mother's "weddin' slippers" to Kathrine; and a photograph of "Gran'mammy" to Ruth: "I was boun' you should remember me; so I jes' went ter de picture man—an' here's my ole black face for you ter keep."—she also reveals in this story her deep love and respect for the Negro mammy who had reared both her mother and her mother's children. The "Gran'mammy" stories are admittedly of prime importance because they suggest many of the influences upon Sherwood Bonner during her formative years; but the power, beauty, simplicity, and truthful presentation of these stories spring from Bonner's deep attachment to her "Gran'mammy."

II *Sweet Girls of Dixie*

The setting of the stories in the second group in the *Suwanee River* is the South during and immediately after the Civil War. Although most of the stories take place in Mississippi, the very first of the four, "A Shorn Lamb," is set in the small town of Guntown, Missouri; and it concerns the successful attempt of Becky Herndon and her mother to disguise a convalescing Confederate soldier, Ned Manning, as a girl in order to protect him from possible capture from unexpected Yankee raiders. There is nothing particularly commendable about the story, for Negro dialect is absent, the plot is obviously a slight one, and the tale undoubtedly belongs more to the tradition of Romance than to either Realism or the local-color movement.

The second story of this group, "C. G.; or, Lily's Earrings," is an amusing and ironic one about how two romantic "sweet girls of Dixie" are duped out of a pair of diamond earrings by a slick confidence man and his wife when the two sisters visit New Orleans. The plot is frail; and, although there is a moral (never trust a stranger), the story is not an interesting one for that reason. It is of some importance in estimating Bonner's ability and rank because it reveals her convincing presentation of other than Negro-dialect tales, since she uses in this narrative the French-Creole dialect of New Orleans. This story also indicates her ability to utilize any setting with which she was familiar and further relates her to the local-colorists. The story also demonstrates Longfellow's interest in Bonner's work, for it contains a French verse written by the poet himself. Sophia Kirk records the poet's interest and contribution in her preface to the *Suwanee River* collection:

More than one bit of literary advice or suggestion I find in the letters of Longfellow to Sherwood Bonner now in my possession. One scrap of paper in the well-known rounded handwriting has on it a few lines sketching the opening scene of a story, in which I recognize Sherwood Bonner's 'Two Storms,' a little romance published in 'Harper's Monthly.' Many of the letters are written in French; and perhaps it is no breach of confidence to tell here that the dainty French poem quoted in 'C. G.; or Lily's Earrings' is from Longfellow's hand. It was published there with his consent, but, at his request, without acknowledgement,—the making of verses in a foreign tongue being regarded as a mere pastime by the poet who was a master in his own.[17]

"Maddy Gascar and the Professor," the third of Bonner's "Four Sweet Girls of Dixie," is the most plotless story in the collection, not excepting the Gran'mammy tales; and it seems to have been conceived with pure humor and satire as its intent. From the title itself to the conclusion, storybook romance and traditional romantic situations (such as the moonlight walk on which the visiting French professor takes one of his sixteen-years-old students) are heavily ridiculed and satirized. With a pairing suggestive of Twain's handling of Tom and Huck, Bonner employs two principal characters, Maddy, the Realist, and Sophronia, the Romantic:

What Sophronia was originally, no one could say; she had read so many novels that she had lost her chance of gaining an individuality. She was like the 'jedge's daughter,' who 'read Novels the whole day long, and I reckon she read them abed.' At school her desk was the abiding-place of tear-splashed volumes, whose contents she devoured in sweet stolen snatches; during her practising hour a paper-back novel would be spread open on the music rack, and her fingers wandered over the keys in strange discords as her soul roved after her hero; when she went out for a walk she took some tale of blood under her arm,—she was as fond of blood in her novels as if they had been race-horses,—and huddled herself under some convenient tree, to weep and read until twilight came, and she could not see another word, even with her nose pressed against the page. The result of all this was that Miss Sophronia was a young lady of a pasty complexion, red eyelids, and uncertain toilet.[18]

The point of view is the first person, but the author intrudes occasionally in parenthetical comments to the reader which inform him that the professor's confidence in his abilities as a lover is to receive a jolt. The French dialect, or accent, is again employed but not so effectively as in "Two Storms." The story was originally published in *Harper's Weekly*, and it was obviously written for the youthful reader of that periodical. It adds nothing to Bonner's stature as a writer, and it is best dismissed as a potboiler.

The last of the stories in this group, "Peacock Feathers," has as its heroine Cecil Anna Carey, who is called Cecil Canary by her friends. Young Miss Carey gets into difficulties at home because she gives as a pledge for ten dollars her grandmother's gold beads worth over four hundred dollars to an old Negro witch of the community who has made for Cecil an ornate, peacock-feather duster to replace one Cecil ruined during her mother's absence. The story suggests the limitless range of Sherwood Bonner's power of creation and invention as subplot moves on to subplot and eventually involves half the community.

The so-called witch woman, Aunt Sini, who has appeared in other stories by Bonner, wears the gold beads to church one Sunday and is promptly arrested for wearing stolen property. Aunt Sini willingly goes to jail, and she respects Cecil's predicament by not revealing that she has been given the beads by Cecil until Cecil is able to pay her the ten dollars. But Cecil quickly learns that Aunt Sini is not moved by pure motives:

> "There is this way," said Cecil. "Of course I shall not let you stay in jail and suffer for me; but as the beads were mine, I can persuade father not to prosecute,—that's what I think it is called,—and you will be released at once."
>
> "An' how 'bout dat ten dollars you owes me?"
>
> "You know I will pay you just as soon as I can."
>
> "An' how much fur holdin' my peace 'bout de whole business? An' how much damages fur dis onrighteous imprisonment?"
>
> "Good gracious, Aunt Sini? do you think I am made of money?"
>
> "Reckin your pa is. Dat's all de same. Plenty o' ways o' gittin' your han's in his pockets."
>
> Cecil sprang up and looked wildly at Aunt Sini, who chuckled like the evil old witch she was.
>
> "Are you proposing to me to steal my papa's money?" she cried.
>
> "Hi! don't be so airy, Miss Flyout! You ain't none tu good, I reckin, wid yo' peacock feathers, an' yo' gold beads, an' yo' miserbul way o' treatin' a frien'less ole nigger lady like me."
>
> Cecil felt as if she should like to whip the "frien'less ole nigger lady."[19]

With a *deus-ex-machina* ending, Bonner arranges for Cecil's father to appear at the jail-house door while the foregoing conversation is taking place; and, with an all's-well-that-ends-well format, Cecil returns to the good graces of the family. From the point of view of theme, or moral, "Peacock Feathers" could just as well have been assigned to the last group of *Suwanee River Tales*, those designed for young readers; but, because of the characterization and plot development and complication, "Peacock Feathers" rightfully completes the second collection of the volume.

III *Tales for the Younger Folk*

The eight stories that comprise the third part of the *Suwanee River* collection, the one jointly entitled "A Ring of Tales for Younger Folks," are in part autobiographical; and they are, as a rule,

exceptionally well-written children's stories. Because they are relatively brief—the longest one is less than twenty pages—they can
hold the attention of even the youngest reader. Moreover, since
they usually contain no more than four or five characters, youthful
readers are not confused by a multiplicity of characters; and the
simple and straight plot line, which has no twists, turns, or subplots,
does not befuddle the child who reads them. The collection certainly suggests that Sherwood Bonner had the ability to write on
several different levels—to adjust her style and technique to the
intellectual attainment of her audience. Most of these eight could be
loosely termed "potboilers." The first, "Tobey's Fortune," is based
upon General Grant's raid on Holly Springs in December, 1862; and
the Tobey of the tale is actually Sherwood Bonner's brother, Sam,
who is only thinly disguised. "Mars Colton's Lesson" reveals how
black and white were reared together prior to the Civil War, and it
suggests that a perpetual bond of love and mutual respect exists
between master and slave and ex-master and ex-slave.

"Dear Eyelashes" is a pleasant, at-times-amusing, at-times-
tender, and always entertaining although sentimental story about
two young children who attempt to help their mother overcome the
handicaps of their present economically depressed situation. The
two children, while playing on the beach near their home, overhear
a wealthy young woman, who is envious of the boy's beautiful
eyelashes, declare to her companion that she would give a hundred
dollars for eyelashes such as his. The next day the two children call
at the home of the rich woman, present her with the boy's neatly
wrapped eyelashes, and respectfully ask for the hundred dollars to
give to their mother, for "there was nothing more to eat" at home.
Naturally, the young woman, deeply touched, as well as amused,
becomes the family's benefactor.

"Rosine's Story," another tale that has the story-within-a-story
framework, is set in Paris during the Prussian attack upon that city
during the Napoleonic Wars. The plot is slight, for the emphasis is
placed on the courageous actions of women under fire, on the effect
of war upon the civilian populace, and on the heroism of those who
die for a cause in which they strongly believe. Despite the setting,
the story has overtones of situations that Bonner has elsewhere
attributed to the Civil War. Perhaps the story should be read as her
deliberate attempt to universalize the bitter suffering of the
civilians—the forgotten victims and heroes of many a war.

The next story of the group, "Leonie," which also uses the story-within-a-story technique, is a personal reminiscence based on Bonner's European tour. The story is interestingly narrated to give the reader an idea of the natural idiom of the speech of the principal characters by employing the "thou" and "thee" translated sense of their native French language. This device is used to convey a feeling of reality, much in the manner of John Steinbeck's rendition in "Flight" of the native idiom of Pepe and his mother. Bonner's story, which is a curious mixture of Realism and sentimentality, centers upon the death of the young and radiant Leonie on the happiest day of her life, her First Communion Day. The sixth story, "The Crest of the White Hat," which has "A Boy's Story" as its subtitle, begins to unfold in Guntown, Missouri, and moves quickly to Andalusia, Louisiana. It is told from the point of view of a young boy at a military school who accepts an invitation from a fellow schoolmate, Henri Dupin, to spend the Christmas holidays with his family. Arrived at the family estate, the boys hear Henri's grandfather narrate the actual story—one about the origin of the family crest, the white hat. Engagingly romantic, this entertaining tale relates how Grandfather Dupin, a young, struggling, unsuccessful hatter became "Hatter to the King," and "fame, fortune, and love followed him forevermore."

The last two tales in *Suwanee River Tales* almost lack any literary merit. "The End of the Dancing-School at Danville" is a completely frivolous story in which the professor of "Maddy Gascar and the Professor" is again presented, but he is now depicted as a French dancing instructor. Since the account concerns an entertaining one of a very young girl's vanity, the story appeals to an extremely limited audience. The last of the "Tales for Younger Folks," "The Finding of Absalom," is set in northern Georgia. The slight plot is based on the disappearance of the young child and his return to his family home through the efforts of a vacationing couple. The story contains a limited degree of suspense and would appeal to youthful readers, but it scarcely belongs in the realm of serious literature.

In summarizing the content and importance of *Suwanee River Tales*, one can justly say that the stories could not sustain their author's reputation. The tales of the third group of stories are no better than thousands of other children's stories that have perished with each passing generation. Nevertheless, taken together, the stories found in *Suwanee River Tales* do suggest that Sherwood

Bonner was always a keen observer of scenes, situations, and people around her and that nothing was lost on her impressionable mind. They display, as previously noted, her unusual ability to spin tales that would naturally engage the interest and attention of young people. This fact should not be surprising since many of the tales she weaves are in fact the very same ones that had interested and amused her as a child.

Quite properly, the allusions found throughout these "Tales for Younger Folks" are not the literary ones that dominate her other stories—allusions to Keats, Thackeray, Shelley, Shakespeare, and Swinburne. Writing on the level of her audience, Sherwood Bonner depends in these tales on references to "Billy Boy and his cherry pie," "Chicken Little and the falling sky," the "Pied Piper," and "Robinson Crusoe." If one of the requirements of a capable author is to address himself to his audience, Bonner surely must be granted this ability.

Suwanee River Tales, however, would not have been reissued during the same year of its first printing; nor would Sherwood Bonner have been the subject of eighteen theses and dissertations in the twentieth century, if she had written nothing more than "A Ring of Tales for Younger Folk." From the beginning of Bonner's career, she has been widely praised for her Realistic portrayal of Negro dialect and for her faithful presentation of character, particularly of Negro characters, and especially that of her "Gran'mammy." Several years before better-known authors were introducing distinctive dialects in their short stories and sketches, Sherwood Bonner was skillfully presenting a character that has become a standard type in American regional literature. Nor is it only nor even wholly Bonner's Realistic Negro dialect that has been responsible for the extraordinary success she achieved in her own time and for the limited recognition she has recently received. Bonner's skill at recreating the scenes, incidents, and settings with which she grew up marked her early for praise; and almost one hundred years later her work is still appreciated for its honest rendition of a culture that has passed:

The bulk of Sherwood Bonner's writing belongs to the local-color genre that burgeoned in the United States during the 1880s; that is, it existed for the primary purpose of depicting the people of a certain locale and their way of life. Her local-color stories did not only depict the life and people of an area, however, but also depicted them realistically recording as accurately as possible not only the dialect spoken but also the way the people acted and the everyday activities in which they engaged. In her Gran'Mammy stories, in "Hieronymus Pop and the Baby," and in "Aunt Anniky's Teeth," for example, Bonner had Southern blacks tell their own stories in their own language and through their own actions. . . . The strength of these local-color stories is found in the natural description, the character delineation, and the humor.[20]

Despite Bonner's success with her local-color stories and her early and usually successful attempts at Realism, even her best stories display some weaknesses. While she had an accurate eye for detail, she frequently allowed excessive detail to get in the way of the story. Thus, in narrating the story "Gran'mammy's Last Gifts," Bonner spends too much time on Ned, "Gran'mammy's" husband, who does not figure in the story at all. Her chief weakness, particularly in the longer stories, is a tendency to invent irrelevant subplots or to have implausible connectives between legitimate incidents in the story, as she does in "Peacock Feathers." On balance, however, the stories and sketches that comprise *Suwanee River Tales* are superior to the repetitive work of a writer like Bret Harte, but inferior to the work of the more important Realistic writers of the 1880s such as James and Howells.

CHAPTER 5

The Uncollected Tales

NOT including the four-part serial, "The Valcours," the uncollected short stories of Sherwood Bonner are seven. The range of these seven stories is extremely wide, for they include inconsequential children's sketches, such as "An Angel in the Lilly Family," a two-page "short-short" aimed exclusively at a youthful audience, and "A Volcanic Interlude," a cruelly Realistic story of miscegenation. The range of these seven stories can serve, however, to show Bonner as a transitional writer who moved from children's stories through Romanticism to Realism and Naturalism. Consequently, the stories in this chapter are grouped according to the probable thematic intent of the author.

I For Children

The first two stories belong wholly to the realm of children's stories, and they were probably designed as much for reading to young children as for reading by young children. The "Terrible Adventures of Ourselves and the Marshall," a first-person point of view story, was published in *St. Nicholas Magazine* in May, 1879. The characters in the story are families of spiders, and their "terrible adventures" consist of trying to get back to their safe quarters in the Meriwether attic after they have left their "home" to watch a nearby fire.

"The Angel in the Lilly Family," which appeared in *Harper's Young People* on October 19, 1880, is a delightfully amusing children's story that again demonstrates that Bonner could successfully direct her energies and talents to any of numerous diverse audiences, but it does not rank as serious literature. Best regarded as a potboiler, it, too, is a short-short—a humorous sketch of the doll family that Sherwood Bonner owned as a child.

II *Romantic Tales*

Two of the uncollected tales are primarily Romantic in content, theme, and execution. A Civil War story, "Miss Willard's Two Rings," was published in *Lippincott's* in December, 1875; and this publication marked the initial appearance of Bonner's work in a quality literary publication. The story is not one of her strongest, largely because of the sentimental ending. The setting is Hollywell, a little town in Northern Mississippi, Bonner's favorite fictional name for Holly Springs. The time is the second year of the Civil War, after the town had been repeatedly subjected to "raids from both armies." The protagonist, Miss Cornelia Willard, freely sacrifices her small store of gold coins to aid an escaped prisoner-of-war make his way back to the Northern lines. He eventually dies as a result of war wounds, but not until he has informed a fellow officer, Harvey Kent, about Miss Willard's generous act and has given him a ring to deliver to her.

Kent returns from the war a hero and a colonel, and eventually finds Miss Willard to present her with the ring which the former prisoner, Jack Hardin, had made for her. Kent ultimately gives Miss Willard a ring of his own, "a large and lustrous diamond," and makes her his bride. The point of view of the story is that of the third person limited. The characters are not carefully drawn, and neither humor nor dialect carries the story through its weak plot. It is easy to see why "Miss Willard's Two Rings" would have been popular to a nineteenth-century, Romantic audience; but the sentimentality of it would lessen its appeal to a more critical and demanding reader.

"Christmas Eve at Tuckyho," the last story that Sherwood Bonner wrote, was not published until seven months after her death, when it appeared in the January, 1884, issue of *Lippincott's*. Set in North Carolina, this story brings still another region under Bonner's scrutiny. In this thorough going story of romance, the opening lines describe Fate as "serene, amiable, and grand"; and, in the closing scene, the narrator-protagonist, Angela Violett, wins forever the heart of her diffident admirer, Cuthbert Gordon. In between, Bonner includes the disappearance of a wayward son and the semitragic tale of a daughter disowned because of an impetuous marriage with, in the eyes of her father, her unworthy tutor. Through Bonner's use of coincidence, the wayward son, Winton Violett, and the disinherited daughter, Lida Erskine, become married lovers. Angela and

Cuthbert, deeply in love with each other, secretly arrange with Winton and Lida to reappear at the Erskine house at Christmas time; in the holiday spirit of love and forgiveness, the son and daughter are reconciled with their respective parents; and the engagement of Angela and Cuthbert is announced.

Admittedly, this plot summary does not do the story justice; for the strength of its characterization suggests the growing competence of Bonner as a skillful portrayer of character. The coincidences, although more frequent than one would reasonably expect to meet in life, are not so overwhelming as those, for example, in O. Henry's "A Municipal Report." The structure of the story is sound; the action glides along smoothly; and, if the ending is inevitable, the way to it is a pleasant journey. It may say something about Bonner's own regard for the story to note that Dorothy Gilligan states that Sherwood Bonner intended to collect it, together with "The Valcours," and "Miss Willard's Two Rings," in a third volume of her stories, tentatively entitled *Romances*.

III *Realism*

The influence and encouragement of William Dean Howells and of the Realistic movement in general probably account for Bonner's move from Romanticism to Realism that is detected in the remainder of her uncollected stories. Published in 1879, 1880, and 1881, at a time when Sherwood Bonner was living in Boston and, as Longfellow's protégé, welcome in literary society, all three of the remaining stories have strong elements of Realism. "The Revolution in the Life of Mr. Balingall," which appeared in *Harper's New Monthly Magazine* in October, 1879, is set during a yellow fever epidemic in the town of Kilbuck, a Mississippi River community located about five miles above Natchez. George Balingall goes to Kilbuck to seek a young woman whom he has seen only once and who is known to him only as Idalia, or "Somebody's 'Idol,' " as George tells himself. When he finds her, she is in mourning for her lover who has died in the plague. Balingall resolves to remain in Kilbuck to win Idalia "back to forgetfulness and a new love." The story is unusual only because it lacks a definite conclusion, but there is little doubt in the reader's mind that George and Idalia will eventually marry. Still, a strong Realistic element appears in the story; for Idalia's fiancé, Fane Evans, is struck down in the prime of his life by the fever. The implication is that one must accept life as it is, the thorn as well as the rose, and that one must hope that all is never totally lost.

"Two Storms," which appeared in *Harper's New Monthly Magazine* in April, 1881, is one of Sherwood Bonner's longest short stories; and this fact may account for its prime weakness: its many parts simply do not form a coherent narrative. Set on the Texas-Louisiana Gulf Coast during and after the Civil War, the war remains constantly in the background but does not touch the lives of the characters. The scene itself never shifts; and, during the time that elapses in the story, approximately twelve years, no or little violence occurs in the physical setting. The weakness is due to Bonner's inclusion in the story of events, people, and situations that have no relationship to each other, or at least not discernible ones such as the hoodoo-voodoo practices of the Negro nurse, Maum Dulcie, and the role of Miss Sims.

In bare outline, the story seems simple enough: it opens with Dina Mabyn's parents horseback riding on the beach while Dina's mammy is regaling the young girl with the well-known fable of "The Tar Baby." When a terrible storm ensues, Mr. and Mrs. Mabyn reach home safely, but an accident directly caused by the storm takes the life of the mother. The distraught husband plunges recklessly into a string of business ventures; and he completely forgets, and thereby neglects, his growing daughter until a second storm, ripping savagely into an off-shore island where his daughter is vacationing with friends, threatens her safety. The storm destroys the lives of many, including those of Belle and Margaret Sims, with whom Dina has been staying. Dina, however, is spared, the father and daughter are reconciled, and they "began a new life, hand in hand."

Despite the obvious weakness of Bonner's attempt to include too much of a diffuse nature, she once again succeeds in including a strong degree of Realism in the story. Dina has an affair with a married novelist, Marion West; and his casual and cruel confession to Dina's father in the young girl's presence—"I loved her. . . . I would have taken her away with me. She seemed to be of no particular value here. And I wanted her. But I am already married"—suddenly confronts Dina with one of the realities of life's conflicts. And at the moment, except for her father, there is no "hero to the rescue," a condition usually found in such contrived situations. In "Two Storms," Bonner again uses Creole dialect and indicates her felicity in the Realistic portrayal of the native dialects of any region in which she had spent an appreciable amount of time. The delineation of character in "Two Storms" suggests that Bonner was becoming more of a careful craftsman in the tradition of Henry James, for one observes a fuller and wholly credible characterization of the story's principals who are individuals rather than types.

This story actually contains enough material for a longer work, either a novel or multipart serial, much like Frank Norris' short story "A Deal in Wheat." While the excessive material has been labeled a basic defect of the story, this narrative also indicates Bonner's growth as a serious writer and perhaps suggests the direction her career might have taken, had she lived. Since all four of her longer works were written during the last half of her short career, this story may indicate that she was tending in the direction of the novel and away from the short story as her most characteristic form; nonetheless, the short story would surely have continued to occupy an important place in her writings.

IV *"Exaggerated Realism"*

The last of the uncollected tales under consideration is one of Bonner's strongest and most Realistic. Indeed, if one accepts a definition of Naturalism as "exaggerated Realism," a definition still acceptable to some critics today, "A Volcanic Interlude," published in *Lippincott's* in April, 1880, may be called Naturalistic. Certainly its coarse Realism approaches that of the early Stephen Crane in *Maggie: A Girl of the Streets* or of Theodore Dreiser in *Sister Carrie*. One of its principal characters, Mr. Dufresne, who is described as one who "led a somewhat roystering life," is more amoral than Dreiser's Hurstwood in *Sister Carrie* or than Crane's Maggie. As a result, the story's publication resulted in the cancellation of several subscriptions to *Lippincott's*.[1]

In the course of the story, it is revealed that none of Dufresne's three daughters, whom he is educating in New Orleans prior to presenting them to Louisiana society, is legitimate. The scene in which Dufresne confronts his daughters with the facts of their mothers' origins has much that would have been considered of shock value even after the turn of the century. One by one the daughters learn the terrible truth concerning their mothers. The initial revelation is that they are not sisters but half-sisters, but this fact is not the bitterest pill that each has to accept:

"My mother," said Irene hoarsely—"who was she?"

"Your mother" said Mr. Dufresne with perfect coolness, "was the daughter of a neighbor's overseer—Mr. Iberville's, I believe. She was pretty, passionate and ignorant. She was eighteen—I twenty. We used to meet in the woods. I took her with me to the city, and we were as happy as a buck and doe in the forest until you were born. Then she was less pretty—and I was twenty-two. She ran away at last—whether to a river or a rival I have never known."

Silence, a terrible silence. Irene's face was like a leprous mask.

Cora's voice broke into the air. "I hope," she said with a burst of sobs, "that at least *my* mother was a lady."

"Oh, indeed!" cried the father with a savage laugh, "she was a balletdancer at the Varieties Theatre. She was exactly like you, and I suppose you call yourself a lady? I got her a house, and lived with her until I was tired of kicking her lovers down stairs."[2]

The parish priest who has been discussing the prospects of Mr. Dufresne's forthcoming marriage with him and who has witnessed the words and scene described above, interrupts Dufresne's narrative at this point:

"This is too horrible!" exclaimed the priest.—"Children, do you not see that there is but one refuge for you?"

"Damn that refuge!" roared Mr. Dufresne.—"He wants to make nuns of you, girls. Now listen to me, you foolish little things. I am getting married entirely for your sakes."

"Pity he had not been so self-sacrificing three times before!" murmured the priest, who was not without a sense of humor. . . .

"Come, dears," cried Mr. Dufresne with the eager charm of manner that was the Dufresne gift, "let us confound all plotters. You are *my* daughters; you shall miss nothing in your lives."

"Ah!" cried a thrilling voice, "we shall miss for ever a mother's love."

It was little Zoe who spoke.

Forgetting her shyness, she ran forward. She clasped in her small brown palms her father's hands: her great eyes, fever-lighted, fixed themselves on his. "Dear father," she said, "tell me of my mother. I have sighed for her always. I have dreamed of laying my head against her heart. Perhaps she still lives, suffering alone. Permit me, father, to pour my love, like scented oil, into her bleeding wounds."

Mr. Dufresne threw up his hand: "Good God, Zoe! where did you learn so much romance?"

At this she withdrew herself, and stood apart with an ineffable and pathetic air of dignity: "Very well, father: I appeal no more to your heart. Tell me plainly of my mother."

At last Mr. Dufresne was embarrassed. He looked at the glowing, angel-like face of his youngest child, and his own colored redly. "Zoe! Zoe!—" he stammered.

"Tell her," said the priest sternly. "Or shall I?"

"Keep it from her," entreated the father.

"That is no longer possible," said Father Marquette. "—Zoe—be brave, my girl—your mother was your grandmother's waiting-maid, a slave. She died, clasping the cross to her bosom, when you were born."

Another silence, more terrible than the first. Zoe drew herself together like a flower that shrinks when the sun goes down. A small stunned creature, she gazed wide-eyed on the priest, whose words had cast her out from the pleasant land of love and hope to an empty and dreadful isolation.

Finally, with a little pitiful moan, she stretched out her hands to her sisters. "Reenie! Cora!" she cried.

But the two girls, hot and shaken with her shame, shrank away.[3]

Two basic flaws appear in this story; and the first is Dufresne's handling of the confrontation scene. His actions, especially the cruel and harsh manner of his revelation, are wholly unrealistic and are inconsistent with his earlier characterization which describes him as being fond of his children and as being solicitous about their well-being: "Their father was Mr. Dufresne, whose name, distinguished in Louisiana annals, glittered now with the wealth that successive generations had accumulated. . . . no one could accuse him of neglecting his daughters; for, apart from his frequent visits, he had more than one summer taken them with him to the Northern lakes and carefully devoted himself to their entertainment. He petted them like little princesses, and they admired him immensely."[4]

The second weakness is the conventional and sentimental final paragraphs in which the scene is revisited after a lapse of fifty years and in which Cora and Irene are described as having made brilliant marriages with the patriarchs of New Orleans' society. And, "as for Zoe, little Zoe, it was her happy fate to die when she was eighteen years old." Apart from the "anticlimactic final paragraphs,"[5] the story is a powerful one, a Naturalistic interpretation of some of the darker aspects of life that were traditionally ignored in the American literature of the nineteenth century, even by those, who, like Howells, defended the rights of others to examine them.

The uncollected tales of Bonner, taken as a group, suggest two directions that Bonner appeared to be heading in at the same time that she was nearing the very end of her short-lived career: her subject matter, incidents, themes, and characters were all tending toward the Realistic and away from the Romantic; and she was moving away from the simple folktale of the regionalist and local colorist to a longer and more complex story with an emphasis on character and with more careful attention to setting and point of view. Two parallels come to mind: the development of the novel as a literary genre, and the movement and direction of Mark Twain. The novel, beginning with Daniel Defoe, initially focused on plot and incident; and almost no attention was paid to organization, unity, and characterization. The writings of Mark Twain moved from the anecdotes and sketches of *Roughing It* in the early 1870s to the Romances of Tom Sawyer in the late 1870s and early 1880s and finally to the book which, according to Ernest Hemingway in *The Green Hills of Africa,* marked the beginning of modern American literature: the Realism of *Huckleberry Finn.*

Just as Twain's movement from local color to Realism can be seen in representative selections chosen from the works just indicated, so, too, can the movement of Bonner be traced by reading the tales that belong to the uncollected group. Indeed, it is difficult to imagine that "An Angel in the Lilly Family" and "A Volcanic Interlude" were written by the same author, and published during the same year, unless one recognizes that "An Angel" belongs to an earlier tradition and that "A Volcanic Interlude" indicates the direction that the fiction of Sherwood Bonner would take during the final phase of her literary career. In the following year, 1881, Bonner published *The Valcours,* a work that confirms her intention during the late 1870s to move away from the short fiction of the local-color school and to embrace the still-emerging Realism of Howells, James, and Twain with its emphasis on the importance of setting, point of view, characterization, and verisimilitude.

CHAPTER 6

The Longer Fiction

I A Novella:"The Valcours,"or"The Goose that Laid the Golden Egg"

"THE Valcours," a four-part serial published in *Lippincott's* from September through December of 1881, is primarily a novel of character. Set in the two cities of Arnville, Louisiana, and Hot Springs, Arkansas, in the years immediately following the Civil War, the story contains seven principal characters—a number that suggests the plan for a short novel rather than the outline for a long short story. The Valcours consist of the General, a product of the antebellum plantation South and now somewhat of an anachronism; his son, Garouche, or Garry, an easy-going, affable, and thoroughly likeable young man who has little to do except manage the surviving Valcour plantation and defend the family honor; and Madame Valcour, a "gay, good-natured, witty, well-bred" woman who is able to control General Valcour's violent outbursts of temper. Early in the novel, using a mixture of metaphorical language and historical references, Bonner describes the General and his son:

When General Valcour rose in his stirrups and made a speech, he knew not "the subtle ways" into which it would lead. In itself the speech was not as bright as a comet's head, but it had a longer tail. . . . The Valcours, father and son, were a noticeable pair. Who has not heard of the Valcours of Louisiana,—the tall, thin, courtly, keen-eyed, polished race? The "fighting Valcours" they had been always called, and in time of war our general did not forget what was due to his name. He had commanded a brigade of "Tigers," whose fame rang through the South. Ill-natured people said that since the war a brigade of tigers had commanded the general. He called them principles: they were otherwise known as prejudices. In truth, he did not easily get over the results of the war. In his broken age the memory of some desperate charge would call blood and fire to cheek and eye. He was in very earnest a "last-ditch" soldier, who grieved sorely that his bones had not been left to whiten on a Southern battle-field rather than he should live to swallow the bitter results of defeat.[1]

The Valcours are soon joined by David Patman Church and by his sister, Buena Vista Church, one of Sherwood Bonner's most inventive and engaging fictional characters. David had recently purchased the Arnville *Avalanche,* a Republican paper whose cartoon illustrations were drawn by Buena Vista, a wily, conniving, scheming but highly attractive young lady who looks out for herself in every instance. To complete the cast of main characters, Bonner has Eva Charenton Leacock and her fabulously wealthy grandmother arrive from New Orleans to relax and enjoy the splendid climate of Arnville.

The dual setting of Arnville and Hot Springs is a rather ingenious device employed by Bonner by means of which she is able to contrive and control the situations and conflicts of her story. Whenever it is convenient to do so, she removes the Valcours to Hot Springs for the sake of the General's health and prepares, during their absence, whatever complications are necessary to keep the plot moving, such as the timely arrivals and departures from the Charenton residence, which adjoins that of the Valcours. Then, when all is ready, a single letter dispatched from Eva and directed to Garry can bring the Valcour clan home to Arnville.

The plot, despite the length of the story and the absence of any appreciable subplot, is not overly complicated. Although Bonner has seemingly placed too many characters on her canvas to permit the development of a single situation, she effectively resolves the central conflict, without leaving any loose ends. Both Buena Vista and Eva Charenton are in love with Garry Valcour. Buena Vista, named by her grandfather in the hope that she would acquire the high spiritedness of her namesake, is the Becky Sharp of nineteenth-century American literature. Cunning beyond measure, she, in her dual role as adviser to both Eva and Garry, easily breaks their engagement by implanting mistrust and doubt in the heart of each.

Buena Vista's scheme to win Garry for herself is frustrated by the death of Eva's grandmother and by the subsequent appearance of Eva's supposed father, an alcoholic and the sworn enemy of General Valcour because of an incident that had happened when the General was in Hot Springs. Buena Vista remains in complete control of the situation, however, until an unfortunate accident to Eva's supposed father, Philip Hamilton Leacock, ruins Buena Vista's plan. Thinking that he is on his deathbed, he confesses that he is not Eva's father but had assumed his identity upon the death of her real father. Eva, released by this revelation from her self-imposed determination not to inflict Leacock on the Valcour family, renews her engagement to Garry. The two lovers marry, Buena Vista goes to Europe to study art at her brother's insistence, and the senior Valcours return to their former life of repose, this time to await eagerly the arrival of their grandchildren.

The story has admittedly some of the elements of a typical nineteenth-century Romance, and Bonner actually intended to rename it *The Goose That Laid the Golden Egg* when she reissued it in a collection of stories tentatively entitled *Romances*. (The "golden egg" refers to Grandmother Charenton's fortune which Eva inherits, part of which Mr. Leacock, as the "long lost father," hoped to gain for himself.) What saves the story, however, is Bonner's careful attention to structure and her consistency of characterization. Although many humorous sayings and situations abound in this story, the characterization of Buena Vista endears the story to its readers. Every perceptive character in the story recognizes her cunning and her shrewd intelligence, but only the alcoholic Mr. Leacock, a confirmed scoundrel himself, sees Buena for what she is—"a double-faced little vixen." The comparison of Buena Vista to Becky Sharp is by no means a fanciful or unjustifiable one, for Buena Vista, with her feigned expression of sympathetic interest in everyone, is able to suggest and insinuate the plot complications that not only keep the story moving but also threaten to destroy the only real love that exists among the younger people, that between Eva and Garry.

All of the principal characters represented in *The Valcours* are vivid and lifelike, and the story indicates what Sherwood Bonner could do with character when the compactness of the traditional short-story format was extended in length. More and more, Bonner became increasingly interested in her later writings in the presentation of character; and the characters in her longer works are as finely drawn as any in the nineteenth century. Furthermore, Bonner, possibly because she was a woman, could do what many of the major writers of the late nineteenth century could not—create effective, Realistic female character portrayals. With the exception of Henry James, no American writer of the 1870s and 1880s could create credible women—surely not Twain, nor Garland, nor Harte; and even the female characters of Howells are pale and lifeless when measured against Bonner's Buena Vista Church.

II *A Novel: A Quasi-Biography*

Like Unto Like, the only novel by Sherwood Bonner published in her lifetime, appeared in 1878. Dedicated to Longfellow, it contains one of the few serious verses that Bonner ever wrote for publication:

> O poet, master in melodious art,
> O man, whom many love and all revere,
> Take thou, with kindly hand, the gift which here
> I tender from a loving, reverent heart.
>
> For much received from thee I little give,
> Yet gladly proffer less, from lesser store;
> Knowing that I shall please thee still the more
> By thus consenting in thy debt to live.[2]

There is little doubt that Sherwood Bonner recognized that she owed to Longfellow's friendship and sponsorship much of the reception accorded her work by the periodical editors. Not only is the dedicatory poem in *Like Unto Like* indicative of this debt, for letter after letter from her to the poet thanks him profusely for his interest in her work and for the introductions he has given her.

All sources agree that the novel is at the least a semiautobiographical one, and Bonner's earlier biographers were unanimous in declaring it to be wholly autobiographical. It is of some slight relevance to note in this connection that Longfellow frequently addressed Sherwood Bonner as Blythe Herndon, the central character of *Like Unto Like*. Most assuredly the setting of the novel, the small Southern town of Yariba in Alabama, is modeled in Holly Springs:

> But the great beauty of Yariba was the Spring. It was indeed one of nature's wonders; an artery from her hidden heart laid bare. . . . it reached a pebbly bed, and wandered away, a placid stream, ever widening, flowing gently through low meadow lands, until it turned into a canal once used for floating cotton down to the Tennessee.
> Yariba people gloried in the Spring. It was something to show to strangers. It was a theme for poets. It was as useful as it was beautiful.[3]

Some inconsistency exists in connection with the setting; for, although Bonner is quite specific in placing Yariba in Northern Alabama, frequent references that occur to Mississippi throughout the novel cause one to feel that the action has been shifted to that state. Bonner's own account of the details of its publication, recounted in a long letter to her father, indicates that, although the novel needed some minor revisions, the editor insisted on printing it as it was when he first read it.

Like Unto Like succeeds primarily as a novel of character, and whether the principal characters are from Alabama or Mississippi makes no difference. They are most assuredly Southern and represent the Southern view toward life. The novel opens with a description of each of the three young ladies who play important roles in the conflict of the novel: Betty Page, Mary Burton, and Blythe Herndon, the protagonist. As the three girls chatter on a bridge about parties and such, Blythe's parents, Lawyer and Mrs. Herndon, approach. They bear the news that Mr. Jim Tolliver, a leading citizen of the community, has agreed to take as boarders Colonel and Mrs. Dexter of the occupational army of the North.

The Dexters' residence in the Tolliver household prepares the way for Bonner to introduce the second principal character of the novel, Roger Ellis, a so-called Northern radical (self-termed, and for different reasons similarly described by the residents of Yariba), who arrives as a summer house guest to visit the Dexters. As Blythe's parents leave, the girls discuss among themselves the effect of the Northern "occupation" on the young ladies of the town. Blythe, when asked if she would allow her sympathy for the North to extend to marriage with a Northern soldier, replies ". . . yes; and further, that I would marry any man I loved—were he Jew, Roman Catholic, Yankee, or Fiji Islander!" When Betty replies that such an action would be treason, Blythe reminds her that "The United States is your country," to which Betty answers "It is not. It is the beautiful, persecuted South."[4] Thus the central conflict of the novel is established early, even before the arrival of the antagonist, Roger Ellis.

Ellis, the self-styled radical, having ". . . helped in the realization of one of his bold dreams—the abolition of slavery in America," takes for his equally monumental task the education or re-education of Southerners in General and of Blythe Herndon in particular:

"Now," said he, laughing, "I call myself a radical thinker; and of course every radical thinker says that man can think out only forms of man—that what the Greeks called Jupiter, and the Jews Jah, or Jehovah, were neither more nor less than their conceptions of ideal manhood. Calling their God the Lord God, and the like, imposes on the multitude, who bow and close their eyes; but to the radical, who stands erect and never shuts his eyes nor his ears, they are only idols—as wretched in the realm of high thought as the South Sea idols are wretched in the world of art."

"I don't quite follow you, Mr. Ellis. I have always thought myself rather liberal in religious matters. I never believed that Cicero and the rest of them went to hell; and sometimes I have even doubted if there could be a place of eternal torment. Yet it is only logical, if you deny that, to deny heaven, isn't it? Oh, how confusing it all is, when one begins to think!"

"Yes, and that is why so few people are willing to think," said Mr. Ellis. "They call themselves conservatives. Conservatism is the creed that teaches that it is better to bear the ills we have than fly to benefactions that we know not of. It is the Song of the Shirt trying to drown the noise of the sewing-machine in the next room."

"And a radical, a true radical, I suppose," cried the young girl, "is one who has thought his way through every tangled problem—whose nature is opened out in every direction like a rose."

"That's a very pretty thought," said Ellis, looking kindly at the fair, bright face. "I don't believe any one before you ever compared a radical to a rose. But, my dear child, there are very few pure types. Every good man has some evil trait, every bad man some good; so every radical has some conservative element in his character. And we are such inconsistent creatures! If a bullet should come whizzing by us this second, I should certainly say Good God! though I might have denied the existence of a God the moment before."

"But you don't quite do that!" said Blythe, under her breath.[5]

Actually, Ellis himself misuses the term "radical"; and, in at least one instance, he does so satirically by considering himself a radical because "I believe in every human soul—and body—having a right to itself."[6] Blythe, on the other hand, is confused with such labels; and she recalls her father's words that only scoundrels and scamps belong to the radical (that is, Republican) party in the South.[7] Later in the novel, when Roger tells Blythe that ". . . when you accepted me you accepted a radical through and through," the term takes on various meanings, depending on who is using it and for what reason. On one occasion, for example, Betty Page refers to Ellis as a radical because ". . . he doesn't make anything of stopping on the street to kiss a black baby."[8]

Hence, to most citizens of Yariba, the term "radical" comes to mean or to suggest unorthodox behavior. Ironically, the most unorthodox and bizarre behavior comes from the most conservative of the Herndons, Blythe's grandmother. Although the elder Mrs. Herndon is but a minor character in the novel, she is one of the strongest and most fully drawn personages Bonner ever depicted. In Mrs.

Herndon's eyes, dancing with the Yankee soldiers and their visitors from the North is immoral; and doing so indicates to her the young people's attitude of forgiveness and reconciliation. She is initially amazed and then outraged when Blythe informs her that she and Roger Ellis are to marry. The grandmother's initial reaction is an attempt to bribe Blythe to reject her lover by promising her the diamond rings and other family jewels that she possesses; then, when Blythe expresses shock at her grandmother's offer and appears more resolute than ever in her determination to marry Ellis, Grandmother Herndon tries to make a pact with God:

> Since the day . . . of Lee's surrender she had ceased to pray; she thought that she had ceased to believe in God. She had gone no more to church, and refused to listen to the ingenious arguments with which Mr. Shepherd, in common with other Southern pastors, tried to excuse God's failure to meet the wishes of the Southern people. But now, as she walked up and down the room with noiseless steps, an old faith stirred within her, mingled with the daring impiety that had grown to be her second nature. In short, Mrs. Herndon was making up her mind to forgive God the past, if he would grant her prayer for the future. She flung herself on her knees by the bed, humbling herself at last, and prayed—prayed that God would do what she could not—prevent this loathed and hated marriage. She pleaded with God for this proof of his power, and promised him her soul as a reward.[9]

The extent of Mrs. Herndon's deep and unreasoning hatred of anything Northern is shown in another scene, one witnessed only by Roger Ellis. Ellis, having discovered that there are several graves of Northern soldiers untended and almost grown over in a remote corner of the town's cemetery, prevails upon Blythe to make him some wreaths to place upon the graves. That same night, Ellis, returning home late from a visit with Blythe, walks past the cemetery and sees what at first he thinks is an apparition: "It reached the flower-covered graves, stooped, lifted a wreath, and the next instant, with a fierce gesture, stripped it of leaves and flowers and threw it to the ground." The figure, of course, is that of Mrs. Herndon, Blythe's grandmother: "Her face was fixed and livid; her eyes wide open; the wind blew her white hair and her white dress gently about her; the diamond on her finger flashed like a little demon's eye. One after another she gathered the wreaths, tore and trampled them."[10]

Despite the occasional bitterness of several of the characters and the relatively slight plot of the novel, *Like Unto Like* is as delightful and entertaining a tale as the majority of Bonner's other stories. The Negro dialect is evident, although naturally it is not so profuse as in the

Gran'mammy tales. Nevertheless, it is just as accurate and just as appealing. In one particular instance of its employment, Civil Rights Bill denies any complicity in connection with a midnight raid on a watermelon patch made on the previous night. He claims that he never left his bed from the time in the early evening he was tucked in until late the next morning; for, as he says, "I don't like ter git broke o'my rest—it stops growin'. Mammy knowd a man onct dat slep till he growed high as de church steeple, an' neber had ter pay nothin' ter go ter de circus 'cause he jes' leaned ober an' looked in."[11]

Included with the dialect is a good bit of humor. At one particular dinner party, the guests are discussing literature in general and Boston, Emerson, Hawthorne, and Concord in particular. Mr. Ellis narrates the "story of a stranger, who, after strolling half a day through a quiet street, seized the first living creature he met—a small boy, of course,—and said, 'Look here, sonny, what do you people do here in Concord?' and the youngster, in the fine shrill voice of youth, replied, "We writes for The Atlantic Monthly!'"[12]

Apart from the central conflict of the novel and the strength of Bonner's characterizations, another interesting aspect of *Like Unto Like*, although irrelevant to the discussion of the merits or faults of the novel, is Bonner's surprisingly modern comment about the American novel that is spoken by Blythe Herndon's father: "What a tremendous thing the man will have to do who writes the American novel! . . . He must paint the Louisiana swamps, the sluggish bayous, the lazy Creole beauties; the Texas plains, with their herds of cattle and dashing riders; the broad, free life of the West, and that of the crowded Northern cities; the skies of California, the mountains of Carolina. Where is the man who can do all this."[13]

As the novel progresses and as Blythe's education becomes more and more complete, the reader discovers that, at least for a while, North is North and South is South, and seldom the twain shall meet. Although Blythe initially proclaims a sympathetic spirit of reconciliation with regard to Northerners in general and to Roger Ellis in particular—"I have no doubt there are gentlemen among the Yankees just as good as there are anywhere; and I should like every house in town to open to them"—and although she initially identifies herself with Ellis' movement—"I should have been an abolitionist had I lived at the North; and, in fact, I think I should have been one even at the South"—Ellis' adoption of a young Negro lad called Civil Rights Bill eventually leads to the first serious quarrel between Ellis and Blythe. When Blythe visits Roger in New Orleans a few months before their marriage is to take place, she discovers Bill, or Willy as he is now called, living with Roger in a father-son relationship. Thus the first hint of trouble during the engagement flares when Blythe asks Roger what role Civil Rights Bill will play in their lives after their marriage. Roger indicates that the couple will make their home in the North and that Bill will accompany them and live in their home:

> "I hope you understand," said Blythe, looking down into her glass, "that I will not sit at table with him?"
> "Blythe—"
> "Please don't let us argue about it," said she, hastily. "I know all that you would say, and my reason tells me that you are right. I agree with you entirely in theory, but—I will *not* sit at the table with Civil Rights Bill!"
> "Blythe, you remind me of the young man who turned upon the girl of his heart, as they sat on the *settle*, spooning sweetly—"
> "How charmingly alliterative!"
> "—With the question, 'Now before this thing goes any farther, I want to know *who* is going to make the fires!' "
> "I suppose I am rather premature," laughed Blythe. "There are more important questions to be settled before—"
> "Before this Civil Rights Bill comes up between us," finished Ellis, with a smile. But Blythe noticed a look of pain succeeded it.[14]

Following the discussion with Roger over Bill, Blythe comes more and more to see that, despite her earlier declarations of independence, she is not quite ready to cast off the creeds in which she had been reared:

> Sometimes she wondered vaguely at herself. "I seem to be crystallizing in a new mould," she said; "or is it that I am just finding out what I really am?" She had been called romantic, but the most romantic expression of love had failed to satisfy her; she had thought herself liberal-minded, but her lover seemed to her a fanatic, and she was not liberal enough to be indifferent to it; she had been impatient of the commonplace, yet she was so commonplace as to desire a smooth and comfortable life; she had openly declared her scorn of "the prosaic and narrow teachings" of her early life, but their influences held her as tenaciously as the earth holds the roots of a flower, while its blossoms may be blown to the winds.[15]

As Blythe considers more and more the future with Ellis, she begins to realize that she is not perhaps so much in love with Roger Ellis as she has been in love with a romantic ideal. Ellis, observing Blythe's growing uneasiness concerning their impending marriage, finally writes to Blythe that he understands perfectly that she may be having second thoughts about their engagement and marriage; and he insists that she give serious thought to their future together, without regard to his personal feelings, and that, if the outcome of such introspection is the decision to break the engagement, he will accept her judgment without argument. Blythe's reply is a masterpiece of expression, as well as a statement of her growing maturity; and she captures beautifully the dilemma that she has faced for the last several months of their engagement:

"Your letter has given me courage to write what is in my heart. I must give you up. I do not love you any more. You will think that I never did, or I could not be so weak as to fall away from you now. I do not know. It is only of late that I have begun to study myself, and I cannot tell whether I have loved you as much as I can love, or whether it was a mistake from the first, and I was simply flattered by your beautiful words, and beguiled by beautiful love. Only this much is now clear to me—that when I think of a future with you, it is with sadness and unrest. I feel like one launching out on a wild sea. I dread your influence over me. I do not wish to turn away from all the sweet teachings of my father and my mother and my early youth. There could be no harmony in our lives. You may be right; but you are at the end of things, I at the beginning. If ever I come to where you are, it must be by my own slow steps. I cannot jump such a space. Since you came South the last time I have had one shock after another.

"I have tried to be faithful to you. I know that you are noble, and nothing shall ever make me doubt that you are true. But I should not know how to live with one who despises what I feel dimly I ought to revere; and who was always running a tilt against things that a giant could not shake. The world is so full of beauty! and the good God who holds it in the hollow of his hand will in his own time turn its evil into good.

"This letter will sound hard, and cold, and cruel; but I cannot help it. I seem to have lost all feeling—but I have suffered. I know the day would come when you, so brillant and advanced, would regret having a wife like me—that is the one comfort.

"I have sinned toward you, but I did not know myself. I know that you will forgive me, and I pray that you may be happy and forget me."[16]

Ellis seems neither surprised nor overly disturbed by his dismissal; and he continues to plan for the salvation, including a Northern education, of Civil Rights Bill. Blythe herself, the reader is told, "young and beautiful and sadhearted . . . sits by her window, and watches ghosts go by, and tells herself that her romance is ended before her life is well begun. Other women than Blythe have made their sad little moans, and have lived to smile at them."[17] That Bonner initially projected additional stories or novels concerning Blythe is suggested by the last sentences of the novel, and the strong possibility is that Bonner planned *The Story of Margaret Kent* as a sequel to *Like Unto Like:* "Wider, deeper, richer joys may wait for her in the coming years, like undiscovered stars that earthly eyes have not yet seen; but I who write, alike with you who read, can only guess at what the future holds—for the story of her life is not yet told."[18]

Although satire is not the strongest element of *Like Unto Like*, there is obviously some attempt on Bonner's part to satirize gently both Northern and Southern points of view. Politics in general are ridiculed by Bonner when she has Blythe declare to study politics as a way of "forming a political creed." She soon discovers, however, that a definition and an understanding of politics depend largely on the speaker at the time. While Roger Ellis speaks, Blythe feels that she is "assisting, as the French say, at an oration." When her father's friends advise her, ". . . more than once she felt like the shuddering little fisherman who uncorked the tight little home in which an ungentle giant was packed away."[19] Blythe also is forced to listen to Roger heatedly declare that "there is no such thing as fanaticism in the cause of truth"; and, on the same day, when she has occasion to object to vicious and heated remarks by one of her father's ultra-democratic friends, he responds, "Why, Miss Blythe, I believe in law and order just as much as anybody; but there are times when a man with a shotgun is of more use to his country than a lawyer."[20] Ellis also at times is bewildered by some of the subtle distinctions between theory and practice. On one occasion, he offers Mrs. Roy, a poor-white widow, a position as head seamstress in Ellis' Black orphan asylum in the North. He cannot comprehend her refusal: "I'll die in my tracks befo' I'll let my children associate with niggers." Yet, when Ellis, puzzled and shaken, leaves the Roy home, he observes the children of Mrs. Roy in the front yard, ". . . who were playing contentedly in the dirt with as many colored companions."[21]

One other incident in the novel also offers possibilities for satire, or even a statement of allegory. After Blythe's rejection of Roger Ellis, he continues to support and educate Civil Rights Bill until Bill is stricken with yellow fever and, after several days of hovering between life and death, dies. While it is tempting to suggest that Bonner is saying that "Civil Rights Bill" cannot live in the South, and to infer all the subtleties of such a symbolic statement, it is probably safer to suggest that, if any symbolic meaning is intended, it is that one cannot exist when removed from his or her environment. In this connection it is interesting to recall Bonner's earlier analogy between Blythe and a native flower: ". . . she had openly declared her scorn of 'the prosaic and narrow teachings' of her early life, but their influences held her as tenaciously as the earth holds the roots of a flower, while its blossoms may be blown to the winds."[22] Thus, the death of Civil Rights Bill should not be blown out of proportion; he is a minor character in the novel who probably serves a two-fold function: on the one hand, he is frequently used to gain humor; on the other, his presence allows Roger Ellis an easy opportunity to practice his "radical" beliefs.

Such economy of character and incident on the part of Bonner is one of the characteristics of her style, and another manifestation of it is her economy of language. Employing much figurative language, particularly similes, metaphors, and analogies, Bonner is able to gain a great deal of meaning from a few well-phrased sentences. She occasionally blends such economical language with humor, as when she comments on her father's aversion to gossip: "Papa never willingly gives gossip any food. I believe he would like for us all to be drowned at sea to avoid the sensation of a funeral in the family."[23] Of the impending break-up between Blythe and Roger, Bonner writes: "It must not be supposed that Blythe Herndon was easily learning to unlove her lover. It was ebb and flow with the tides of her heart."[24] With an allusion to the seventeenth-century *carpe diem* verse, and an interesting reversal of a natural process, Bonner writes early in the novel of the relationships between the young women of Yariba and their male counterparts: "As for the girls themselves, expecting to marry as confidently as they expect a coming birthday, they stave off serious declarations as long as possible, and gather roses while they may; for, once married, their day is over, and they reverse nature's order by becoming caterpillars after they have been butterflies."[25]

In yet another example of Bonner's economy of language, when Betty Page tells Blythe of Betty's engagement to one of the Northern soldiers, Captain Silsby, Blythe asks Betty if she really loves him: "Oh, I love him well enough—not madly, you know. I'm not romantic. But then, neither is he. He isn't a poem-writer, like your Mr. Ellis—but I'm not a poem-reader. We *suit* each other, don't you see, Blythe? and there's everything in that."[26] Lastly, one of Bonner's finest expressions in the novel, combining both allusion and simile, occurs at the novel's conclusion. After Blythe writes Roger, breaking their engagement, Bonner writes that ". . . never again will she know the fresh, ethereal madness that, like the Holy Ghost to the kneeling Virgin, comes but once to the human heart, and is called first love."[27]

In summary, one has to say that *Like Unto Like* is not a great novel but that it possesses some very fine and distinctive characteristics. As Nash Burger has pointed out, "The whole struggle of social and political interests in the South during Reconstruction is brought into the novel and treated with an honesty and a realism that were wholly lacking in Southern literature before the war."[28] The real strength of the novel lies in its creation of character; for, when even the acknowledged masters of the novel such as Twain and Howells were finding it difficult to create effective and credible female characters, Bonner was able to create in *Like Unto Like* two memorable women in Blythe Herndon and her grandmother. The minor characters also come across realistically, whether they are type characters, such as Mrs. Roy and Civil Rights Bill, or supporting characters, such as Betty Page and Blythe's mother and father. Not only is Bonner Realistic in her character portrayal, but she is also wholly Realistic in the execution of the plot of the novel. There is certainly no happier-ever-after ending, and yet the drifting apart and the ultimate breaking up of Blythe and Roger avoid any hint of sentimentality or Romantic self-pity. The death of Civil Rights Bill is additional evidence of Bonner's intention to treat her subject matter realistically. Certainly, the Romantic expectations at the novel's conclusion are denied by the events depicted; and Bonner continues in *Like Unto Like* along the path toward Realism that she had embarked upon early in her career.

There are, however, two legitimate criticisms of the novel that can be made: a hasty conclusion and a slight plot. The novel appears to end too abruptly; although the breaking of the engagement is well anticipated and evolves naturally, Bonner ends the novel too quickly after Blythe's letter of rejection to Ellis. In Bonner's defense, it should be pointed out that, in her letter to her father in which she narrated the events leading up the publication of *Like*

Unto Like, she wrote that the novel ". . . has never been read over since it was written, and some of the chapters are as rough as can be—yet they did not want me to touch it again! Seemed quite reluctant to give it up. I was writing the last chapter when Joseph Harper came for it—and had a fearful time getting it finished, sewing it together and tying it up with the help of the St. James hallboy, while the great magazine was waiting below. I am sure no book was ever before put into their hands under such circumstances."[29]

Not all of Bonner's critics agree that the slight plot is a weakness, and some of her biographers have vigorously defended it. Burger writes that "this very simplicity of plot was one characteristic of the post-bellum realistic movement, and a very real advance on the turgid complexities of ante-bellum romantic narrative."[30] In praising the Realism of the novel, he also notes that "the plot itself steers sharply away from the conventionally romantic" by having "the romance of the principal characters wrecked because of their inability to adjust their lives" to each other. "To Sherwood Bonner, the novel was a valuable lesson in the use of her materials and in the development of her art."[31] Nevertheless, the plot does remain slight; and, without damage to the subject matter, Bonner could easily have increased the role of some of the minor characters and added some meaningful plot complications in order to gain a fuller novel and a more complete treatment of the Reconstruction Era in a small town in the rural South.

III *A Problem: An Autobiography?*

With the consideration of *Like Unto Like,* all of the fiction that can be attributed with certainty to the pen of Sherwood Bonner has been discussed; but one more work needs consideration. The novel, *The Story of Margaret Kent,* presents to the literary historian of Bonner's life and works a problem that is not readily resolved; indeed, the final answer to the questions raised by the publication of *The Story of Margaret Kent* must still be discovered. This novel was published in Boston, in 1886, by Henry Hayes, a pseudonym for Mrs. Ellen W. (Olney) Kirk. Mrs. Kirk was a sister-in-law to Sophia Kirk, who was Bonner's companion in her last several months; and she was also the court-appointed guardian of Lilian McDowell, Sherwood Bonner's only daughter. Without the slightest doubt, the heroine of the novel, Margaret Kent, is a fictionalized version of Sherwood Bonner. Oscar Fay Adams' statement in *Dictionary of*

American Authors flatly declares that "In Mrs. Kirk's novel of 'Margaret Kent' she (i.e., Sherwood Bonner) figures as the heroine";[32] and even a cursory examination of the novel reveals far too many parallels between the lives of Kent and Bonner to allow for any other conclusion.

The question about the authorship of *Margaret Kent* is, however, a different matter. Dr. George Stephenson, Sherwood Bonner's great-grandson, believes that *Margaret Kent* was actually written, or at least begun, by Sherwood Bonner herself. It is a well-known fact that Bonner refused to take any pain-easing drugs during her final illness because she felt that they would interfere with the progress of her latest novel. However, no trace of any unfinished novel by Bonner was ever turned up by any of the Bonner family descendants. Stronger evidence than family suppositions exists, however, to verify the contention that Bonner was in fact working on a second autobiographical novel at the time of her death; for Sherwood's aunt, Martha Bonner, testified during the custody trial for Lilian after Sherwood Bonner's death that Sherwood left "other literary works [from which] we expect to realize more than enough to pay off the Davis mortgage," a mortgage in the sum of $590.[33]

Sophia Kirk's testimony at the same trial is more detailed, for she refers specifically to four items from the sale of which Sophia and Martha hoped to realize enough money to substantiate their claims that they were financially able to care for Lilian: (1) "one more book, which is to come on the market at Christmas time," a reference most probably to the second collection of short stories, *Suwanee River Tales*, which actually appeared early in 1884; (2) a short story, "worth from $100. to $150," a possible reference to "Christmas Eve at Tuckyho," published by *Lippincott's* in January 1884; (3) "a book published in March—can't estimate its value"—which is obviously *Dialect Tales;* and (4) a "book nearly completed, it being so far advanced that another party can complete it. The work will be worth not less than $300., perhaps $400. or more."[34] This last item leads one to consider the possibility that *Margaret Kent* may actually have been begun by Sherwood Bonner.

The inspiration for *Margaret Kent,* if Bonner is the author, might have come from Longfellow. Sophia Kirk, in her preface to *Suwanee River Tales,* notes in discussing *Like Unto Like* that "throughout her career she received the most generous encouragement from the poet Longfellow, who believed in her talent, and did all in his power to forward it. At his insistence she wrote her first novel . . . with a dedication to the poet, who was warm in its praise." This sentence suggests that Bonner, in writing *Margaret Kent*, may have been following Longfellow's earlier advice: "He had at first urged her to throw upon a broader canvas some of her more recent experience, but after hesitating a little, Sherwood Bonner decided to keep to the ground she knew best, and in her heart loved best."[35] It may well be that Bonner felt confident enough, after the general acceptance accorded *Like Unto Like* and her shorter fiction, to follow Longfellow's suggestion and to write a longer work about "some of her more recent experience."

While the internal evidence as to the authorship of the novel is not conclusive, the details revealed about Bonner's marriage and separation strongly suggest that, if Bonner herself were not the author, she surely must have confided much about herself to the author. Since no evidence exists that suggests a direct link between Ellen W. Kirk and Sherwood Bonner, it is reasonable to assume that Ellen Kirk's source of information must have been Sophia Kirk, the only confidante common to both Bonner and Ellen Kirk. And Sophia Kirk's source, in turn, could easily have been "the book nearly completed," and the "notes in her own (i.e., Sherwood Bonner's) hand to complete" that were alluded to in the Lilian custody trial.

The evidence that equates the lives of Sherwood Bonner and Margaret Kent is conclusive enough. Early in the novel, Margaret Kent says of her husband, Robert, that they had known each other all their lives: "Our plantations adjoined each other. [But he] never courted me at all. We had incessantly quarrelled, for we were both egotists, who thought the world existed for our sakes. We had never been the least in love with each other."[36]

In the diary of 1869, the year of her engagement to Edward McDowell, Bonner alludes frequently and with considerable detail to the misunderstandings and quarrels that marred their engagement period; and she even suggests on occasion that she was not actually in love with Edward. The situation outlined at the beginning of *Margaret Kent* closely follows that of Bonner's own life about the time of her death when she would have been working on the novel; for Kent is living in New York with her daughter, Gladys, then about eight years old, and has been separated from her husband for the past six years. After Sherwood Bonner with her daughter Lilian left Edward McDowell in 1873, she struggled tirelessly to make a living for the two of them with her pen, as did Margaret Kent. Margaret, in physical appearance, "was above the ordinary height of women"—Sherwood Bonner was in fact about five feet, ten inches tall—and had "a Southern voice, rich and sweet . . . for Mrs. Kent was an Alabamian." Bonner was, of course, also a Southerner, although from Mississippi.

Numerous other indications suggest that the life of Margaret Kent parallels closely the life of Sherwood Bonner. Margaret shares her New York apartment with another writer, Sarah Longstaffe; and the two have recently completed a European tour together. Bonner and Louise Chandler Moulton, also a writer, had likewise toured Europe together. On the subject of marital situations, Margaret confesses to a friend that she sometimes wonders if her friends believe she is indeed married, for they have never seen her husband: "I've had to vouch for his existence for six years." Bonner undoubtedly must often have felt the same way; for, from her arrival in Boston until the fall of 1878, none of her Northern acquaintances ever saw her husband. Furthermore, Margaret's husband, Robert Kent, is described as having "taken possession of his wife's inheritance, invested it at once in schemes from which nothing had ever been realized." As a consequence, "Margaret had supported her little girl and herself all these six years."[37] The character of Robert Kent so closely resembles that of Edward McDowell and the revelations of this character are so fully detailed that the information could scarcely have come from anyone other than Sherwood Bonner herself.

One instance is recorded in *Margaret Kent* in which Robert uses his daughter's small store of birthday money: "If I take it, it is a mere loan, which I will soon repay. Not only repay, but put in two gold pieces for each one that I take out. I shall soon have money—plenty of money. This is a mere inconvenience."[38] Although the logic and the rationalization remind one strongly of Edward McDowell, an even more marked parallel appears between Kent and McDowell. In an unusually candid moment, Kent admits—as Edward implied both in letters and in direct courtroom testimony—that he often sought, but never attained, the golden touch: "I'm an unlucky fellow. It's always been hard time with me. The moment I ever undertook any business or any speculation, the bottom falls out. . . ."[39]

During Lilian's custody trial, when asked his occupation, Edward McDowell replied that he was "what might be termed a speculator." The final link between Kent and McDowell is suggested by the advice of a relative to Margaret Kent that she should go out west, where she was not known, and obtain a divorce from her philandering husband.[40] Sherwood Bonner had in fact gone to Benton, Illinois, in order to establish residence for her divorce from Edward McDowell.

Bonner, McDowell, Lilian, and Aunt Martha are not, however, the only recognizable persons in *The Story of Margaret Kent*. A strong similarity exists between the description of Herbert Bell of *Margaret Kent* and Henry W. Longfellow. The description of Mr. Bell recalls the poet: "Mr. Bell stood waiting for them as they drove up, with his head bare. He was a man of seventy, tall, and still erect, his hair white as snow, but his brown eyes as serene and brilliant as they had been in youth. He was known in the world as a great poet, but was a simple and kind-hearted old man, with much of the boy about him still."[41] That Herbert Bell was to Margaret Kent what H. W. Longfellow had been to Sherwood Bonner is suggested by the following excerpt:

There was nothing in the world of which she felt so secure as of Mr. Bell's friendship, his affection, even. It was in this very room she had first seen him, years before, when she had come, her heart in her hand as it were, to show him a poem and ask him if he thought anyone would be likely to print it and give her money for it. And his help then and his never-ceasing goodness since had been one of the substantial helps of her life. He was more to her than her own conscience; she trusted him absolutely.[42]

The description, early in the novel, of Margaret's first arrival in the East from her home in the South also suggests that the life of Margaret Kent follows closely the life of Sherwood Bonner: "Margaret Kent had come to New York some five or six years before, almost an absolute stranger; and the acquaintances she made had almost invariably come from accidental collision, in which sympathetic impulse counted for little or nothing. She had written a series of 'Letters from a Southerner,' which had found favor among the readers of a weekly paper, and the flatteries of the editor had been her chief encouragement to try to make a living by literature."[43] It seems unnecessary to point out that Sherwood Bonner's

initial efforts at a literary career also consisted of a series of article-
letters that she wrote for the Memphis *Avalanche*, describing celebrations, sights, and interviews in Boston and the Northeast.

The suggestion that Sherwood Bonner may have been the author
of *The Story of Margaret Kent*, or at least may have written the
original draft of the novel, is not made with the intent of suggesting
plagiarism by Ellen Kirk. Undoubtedly any royalties that the book
earned at the time of its publication were used for the support of
Lilian; for, after the death of Aunt Martha Bonner, Lilian accompanied Sophia Kirk to her home in Pennsylvania.[44] The decision to
publish the book under the name of Kirk rather than Bonner could
have been made for one of two reasons: the book might not have
been as completed as Sophia Kirk felt it was in 1883, and extensive
work had to be done on it by Kirk, who therefore deserved the
credit. Or, since Ellen Kirk, under the name of Henry Hayes, had
already about one dozen titles to her credit, it might have been
believed that a book by her would bring a larger sale than one
bearing Bonner's name. Regardless of the final conclusion reached
concerning the authorship of *The Story of Margaret Kent*, the book
can profitably be read as a semiautobiographical novel about Sherwood Bonner, thus enriching the information presently known
about Bonner's life, especially her relationship with Henry W.
Longfellow and the circumstances of her marriage to Edward
McDowell.

In reviewing the writings of Sherwood Bonner, one is impressed
by the number of times that the name of Henry Wadsworth Longfellow appears. The exact nature of Bonner's relationship with Longfellow constitutes one of the few unanswered questions concerning her
life, but one has no doubt about the poet's literary influence on the
nature, content, and the direction of Bonner's work. Sophia Kirk
details some of Longfellow's specific recommendations to Sherwood
Bonner in her preface to *Suwanee River Tales*. "More than one bit of
literary advice or suggestion I find in the letters of Longfellow to
Sherwood Bonner now in my possession." Kirk states that Longfellow outlined the plot for "Two Storms" and wrote many of the
poems that appear in Bonner's work, including the French poem
quoted in "C. G.; or, Lily's Earrings."[45] In *The Story of Margaret
Kent*, Herbert Bell, the "world renowned poet" who is obviously
modeled on Longfellow, confides to his nephew as to what he has
done to help Margaret Kent (that is, Sherwood Bonner) in her liter-

ary career: "I have used some small influence in getting her poems accepted by magazine editors, and in creating an interest in her stories."[46] In the same novel, Mr. Bell speaks directly to Margaret Kent concerning her ability and the future of her professional career: "'You are a poet,' said Mr. Bell, 'although you are not exactly an artist. You have plenty of the artistic feeling; but an artist is actually a person who knows his trade well—who has an absolute mastery of processes. He may do the thing by a flash of inspiration, or he may do it by painful and careful labor, but he does it in the best way. You will have to work harder over the purely mechanical part before you are a master of your profession. Study that with perseverance and energy.'"[47] Undoubtedly, Bonner profited enormously from such accurate and well-intentioned advice.

One has little doubt that the early local-color stories and the later Realistic ones of Sherwood Bonner owe much to Longfellow's suggestions. In this regard, Longfellow was to Sherwood Bonner what William Dean Howells was to Stephen Crane. Although Longfellow knew that it was too late in his career to change the emphasis of his own work, he saw in Bonner a promising figure who could contribute much to the already developing Realistic tendency in American literature. This recognition may explain why an anonymous reviewer in *Harper's Weekly* could write, following the death of Sherwood Bonner, that "Longfellow, in the decline of his years, seemed to see in her the renewing of his youth, and he did not hesitate to declare that she would be *the* American writer of the future."[48]

Sherwood Bonner learned well from her tutor. Perhaps the greatest service Longfellow performed for her was sending her the Boston newspapers and the leading periodicals of the day. If he had done nothing more for Bonner, he still would have aided her career. Sherwood Bonner had always been a voracious reader, and she became under Longfellow's guidance a more disciplined one as well. Her writing attests to her familiarity not only with the classics of English literature but also with the work being written by her contemporaries. Thus, in *Like Unto Like*, she makes repeated allusions to Ben Jonson, Shakespeare, Burns, Shelley, Keats, Swinburne, Thackeray, and George Eliot. In a brief section in the novel about Hawthorne, Roger Ellis particularly recommends *The Scarlet Letter* to Blythe Herndon: "It will mark a date in your life. I do not know whether I could be so greatly moved again as I was when I first read the 'Scarlet Letter.' Never did a book so profoundly impress my imagination. I have thought since then that it is the matchless flower of American Literature. I was quite young when I read it, but I half fear to read it again, as it seems to be a law of life that the same delight shall never be tasted twice by the same lips."[49]

In *The Story of Margaret Kent*, the steady succession of literary allusions continues, and many of the references are to contemporary writers. Thackeray is quoted liberally on two separate occasions, Browning is discussed and quoted at great length in a conversation between Herbert Bell and Margaret Kent, and Margaret recalls that "she had read Wordsworth's 'Ode to Duty' with a genuine uplifting of soul." The short stories of Bonner also contain repeated literary references, specifically to Samuel Johnson's *Rasselas*, Keats' "Endymion," and Shakespeare's *The Tempest*. It would be foolish, of course, to suggest that Sherwood Bonner first met many of these writers and characters in her Boston reading through Longfellow's recommendations, but the directed reading of her early Boston years was surely responsible to some degree for her lively interest in contemporary literature. Very probably the later Realistic stories of the Illinois prairie and Tennessee-Kentucky mountain region were influenced by the new doctrine of Realism as it was promulgated by Howells and James. It is known that she read James' *The American* in the pages of Howells' *Atlantic*, one of the periodicals that Longfellow sent to her. The letter-articles that she wrote for the Memphis *Avalanche* and Boston *Times*, in which she describes the well-known Boston men-of-letters such as Holmes, Longfellow, Howells, and Lowell, also afforded Bonner opportunities to study these writers and their works and therefore allowed her to anticipate some of the rapidly approaching or developing movements and trends.

CHAPTER 7

Estimate and Conclusion

IN attempting to suggest Sherwood Bonner's place in American literature, one is faced with the difficulty of assessing the worth of material written over eighty years ago with very few guidelines available except comparison and the opinions of those of her own era. Since the opinions of a writer's own generation should not be ignored, the critical comments of Bonner's contemporary reviewers are of some relevance in assessing her rank. Fortunately, largely because of Bonner's friendship with Longfellow, *Like Unto Like* was extensively reviewed when it was published and, in one instance at least, by a literary man of some reputation, Paul Hamilton Hayne. Hayne, in a rather long review—it ran to almost three thousand words—for the Louisville Sunday *Argus*, attacks the novel on moral grounds but praises its literary accomplishment:

'Like Unto Like' is said to be the first production of a Southern lady, 'one to the manor born,' and the story proposes to give some truthful pictures of Southern society, both in the upper and lower classes, since the termination of the war. That this novel is very clever, sometimes brilliant, I can not deny; but there is throughout it a subtle yet all-persuasive undercurrent of sentiment and feeling rising once or twice to the surface, which proves that the writer's sympathy for her own people (if, indeed, she be a Southernor) is disposed to show its light upon decidedly the *'lucus a non lucendo'* principle. Touches of vivid characterization, tragic and humorous, are often recognized; but how a Southern woman, one Southern in principle, could have patiently conceived such a personage as Roger Ellis, or, at least, lingered with such apparent pride, satisfaction and delight over many traits of his ultra Radical nature, and many expressions of his ultra Radical belief, seems to be utterly unaccountable.[1]

Hayne then painstakingly documents his charge against the author, which amounts in substance to calling her a traitor to the South,

137

both by summarizing at great length the content of the novel and by freely quoting from several of the long conversations between Roger Ellis and Blythe Herndon. Toward the conclusion of his review, Hayne returns to a discussion of the literary merits of the novel:

Regarded purely as a literary performance, this work, as I have before intimated, is exceedingly clever; in certain particulars even brilliantly able. The descriptions of scenery, which in most novels bore one unspeakably, are here vivid, picturesque, and truthful, with occasional displays of bright poetic enthusiasm; and of the *dramatis personae*, some are portrayed with quiet but significant humor; some with keen, ironic shrewdness, and one at least (the 'Grandmother of Blythe Herndon') with a degree of tragic force decidedly impressive. . . . Our author's humor is genuine, above all, when it depicts the lower class of Southern whites! Here again a certain lack of sympathy and toleration may be noticed; but the portraits of Mrs. Roy, of Zaraba, and her kind, seem to me very effective. And how life-like are Miss Betty Page and her amorous Lieutenant Silsby; the former sparkling, *espiegle*, candidly selfish; the notion of 'the world well lost for love' being to her merry, sensuous, shallow nature the most absurd of mortal maxims; the latter—heavens! have we not beheld him on parade and off it; quick and firm of step, but slow and uncertain of thought; 'the gloss of (military) fashion and the mould of (military) form'; the adored of younger sisters, and the 'apple' of a doting mother's eye; terrifically stiff in backbone and moustache, unutterably soft in heart and head.
. . . From all this my readers will understand that the fault of 'Like Unto Like' is moral, not intellectual or artistic. Regarded as the performance of a Northern writer, it would be perfectly natural, perfectly comprehensible and blameworthy (in the sense indicated), only so far as prejudice, hasty judgment and the bitterness of sectional dislikes are blameworthy, whether covered by the subtle inference or open, undisguised abuse. Regarded as the performance of a Southern writer, it repels, at all events, the Southern reader. Nor can the great cleverness of the story excuse that irony of deduction and inference which show that the author has been long 'yearning towards the tents of the Aliens.'[2]

In a spirited answer to Hayne's review, R. W. Knott, writing in the same paper, objects to Hayne's thesis, particularly to his discussion of the role of Roger Ellis. Knott begins by declaring that the novel is "quite remarkable for two things: first, for the real talent displayed in the portraiture of character, and then for the entire freedom from partisan prejudices." The review continues in a more specific vein: "Paul Hayne, one of the few men of the South who can wear undisputed the name of poet, reviewed this book in the *Argus* some weeks ago. He was compelled to admit that it was very clever, at times brilliant," but, Knott adds, Hayne objected strongly to Bonner's handling of Roger Ellis, the radical reformer of the novel. For his part, Knott felt that the characterization of Ellis was one of Bonner's strongest:

> Now, the truth is, Ellis has very many idiosyncracies which would plainly unfit him for making a woman happy. But it is decidedly one of the strongest, most personal, actual, individual characters in American fiction. The Grandmother, Mr. Hayne admits, is 'portrayed with a tragic force decidedly impressive,' but he condemns the work, as he says the Southern sympathies of the writer are not strong enough. He says: 'From all this my readers will understand that the fault of 'Like Unto Like' is moral, not intellectual or artistic. . . .'
>
> This book and this criticism seem to represent the power of, and the danger to, Southern literature. There is a disposition among the educated classes to narrow and prejudiced views of art. There is a failure to recognize its high mission, and it would limit the illimitable. Literature can never progress under such conditions. Party feelings, or even the deeper and better feeling—regret for the lost cause—can not control the author's writing for the multitude beyond the parties. Liberality is needed elsewhere as much as on the press or in the Legislative halls. Great artists may attempt—they should attempt—to picture the ten years of reconstruction in the South, for it is a period full of dramatic interest. But it is vain to condemn the performance because it does not accord with the resolutions of '98, or to ostracise the author because she recognizes the soul of good in things evil, even when that evil is personified in a man who might be . . . one who loved his fellow-man when that man was a negro.[3]

Numerous other unsigned reviews attest to the strength of Bonner's performance in *Like Unto Like*. An anonymous reviewer writing for the Boston *Advertiser* called the novel "a very bright book,"[4] and one in the Portland *Press* considered it "one of the most original, brilliant and natural novels of the day; and from certain delicate traits of thought and expression, it is difficult not to trace the authorship to Mr. Sidney Lanier."[5] The St. Johns, New Brunswick, *Globe* reviewer described it as "a brilliant and exceedingly interesting story of life in the Southern States since the war. . . . The style of the writer is attractive, exhibiting as it does the product of a well stored mind, combined with effective expression, the dialogues being remarkable for their sprightly vivacity."[6]

The Boston *Courier's* review was so flattering as to be suspect:

"Sherwood Bonner's new novel in Harper's Library of American Fiction is a book so original, so charming, so complete in itself, that to write a review of it must be one of the most disheartening tasks possible. Not for many years has there been produced a novel so broadly American, so unprovincial while yet retaining the peculiar atmosphere of locality. Its art is so good and so fresh that it hardly impresses us as art; it is more nearly nature."[7] The reviewer continues to discuss the book in great detail, and compares its author with George Eliot. Although this review is one of the few that singles out the defects as well as the virtues—"We, of course, see faults in it. . . . The freaks of fancy and metaphor sometimes verge on extremes"—the concluding comments praise highly Bonner's achievement: "The main thing to observe is that Sherwood Bonner has seized the transition period of the feeling between South and North so perfectly that her book will probably stand in the future as the best representative of this episode in the national life."[8]

Sherwood Bonner's contemporaries were not alone in their generous praise of her talents. In *Southern Writers*, Professor William Malone Baskerville in 1903 considered Bonner to be "the first Southern writer to use negro character with artistic effect in literature."[9] B. M. Drake, praising the reality of her settings and characters, noted that "every experience of her life seems to have furnished her material for literature and she always chose phases of life which she knew thoroughly for the background of her work."[10] Drake also suggested that Bonner's later work gave every indication of artistic perception and professional growth: "In 'Two Storms,' written in later years, the plot is very well managed; and a study of that story will justify the inference that Sherwood Bonner was gaining mastery of her material."[11] To Drake, Bonner's supreme contribution to the literature of the nineteenth century lay in her powerfully appealing humor:

Humor has been called Sherwood Bonner's greatest gift. It pervades and colors her whole work. She runs the whole gamut from the well-turned pun or the mere perception of comicality to the point where humor passes into pathos as we catch a glimpse of the more serious incongruities of life. It was this gift which especially fitted her for dialect-writing. Dialect is the outward and visible sign of the circumscribed life of the provincial. It has always its pathetic and its humorous side; and the written dialect, if it is genuine, must reflect one or both of these, or else, no matter how accurate it is phonetically, it can be of no literary or human interest. Although it may be granted that Sherwood Bonner's dialect is not always phonetically accurate, and it is not always even consistent, yet it is true that she has caught the spirit of the dialect and uses it for its legitimate purpose, to reveal the life of which it is the exponent. In this she perhaps has no superior, and not more than one equal, among the Southern dialect-writers of the last thirty years.[12]

In many of her stories, Bonner utilizes a technique similar to that employed by Joel Chandler Harris and other writers of her time— the framework of the tale within the tale. In this technique, as well as in her use of humor and dialect, Bonner reveals the debt she owed to the writers of the Southwest school of humor, as well as to Mark Twain. Frequent references occur to Twain in her stories, and at least one of her letters from Europe is written in precise imitation of the style and the method of satire that Twain uses in *Innocents Abroad*. Professor Alexander Bondurant also felt that Bonner's principal contribution to American literature was as a writer of local color:

She probably wrote the first story of any writer that belongs to the distinctively Southern school. She wrote before '77 some of 'The Gran'mammy Stories,' and these seem to be the first negro dialect stories published in a Northern journal, and thus speaking to the whole country. She wrote in '78 'Like Unto Like,' a story that has to do with the reconstruction period. Into this field Cable came later, and Page selected it as a fitting period in which to locate his most ambitious work, 'Red Rock.' Only one writer before her had attempted to work this virgin soil, Baker in 'Colonel Dunwoodie, Millionaire.' In this book she refers to the 'Tar Baby Story,' which she published several years later in *Harper's Monthly*. She wrote some excellent dialect stories of the Tennessee mountains, thus doing pioneer work in a field which Miss Murfree has made so peculiarly her own. She spent some time (beginning in 1880) in that portion of Illinois known as Egypt; and 'On the Nine-Mile,' and 'Sister Weeden's Prayer' illuminate this dark world. These stories and a number of others were written in the dialect peculiar to this region. Of 'Sister Weeden's Prayer' in the 'new' dialect *The Nation* spoke in most complimentary terms. She seems to have been the first to give to the vernacular of this region literary treatment, thus doing for Illinois what Eggleston and Riley have done for Indiana.[13]

One of the few recent estimates of Bonner's work is contained in Edward Wagenknecht's *Longfellow: A Full-Length Portrait* (1955), where he describes Sherwood Bonner as a "somewhat daring writer in her time," and concludes his estimate of her work with a comment about *Like Unto Like*: ". . . it is certainly a work of sufficient promise to make it reasonable for us to believe that, if she had lived, she would certainly have realized at least a reasonable measure of her high literary abilities."[14]

It is of some relevance in this overview of Sherwood Bonner's place in American literature to recall that the author of *Like Unto Like* was compared with George Eliot, Jane Austen, and Sidney Lanier. Furthermore, her finely drawn characterizations suggest the influence of Henry James; and, as has been noted, Bonner had read James' *The American* during her Boston apprenticeship. Assuredly, Bonner was no George Eliot and most certainly no Henry James; but the strength of her character portrayals in her later writings suggests that she had learned well during her literary apprenticeship and beyond and that she understood, along with many of the then-emerging youthful Realists, the importance of character in fiction. If being in Boston with Longfellow was being in the right place at the right time, her learning technique from James and Howells was a tribute to her own capacity to learn and to grow as a story teller and a maker of character.

Mark Twain, in his preface to *Huck Finn*, takes pride in explaining to his readers his use of a number of dialects throughout the novel; and critics from Howells to Hemingway have praised Twain for his variety and verisimilitude with regard to dialect. In Bonner's employment of dialects and their variations (from that of the Mississippi Negro to the Tennessee mountains to the Louisiana French to the Southern Illinois), she exhibits a knowledge and a familiarity that was exceptional in its day. Gifted American authors like Cooper, Hawthorne, Melville, Brown, and others of less importance, such as Harte and Harris, generally had all their characters, both within a story and from story to story, speaking alike. Bonner clearly distinguished the speech patterns of her characters, and she cleverly employs setting and locale to reinforce her handling of dialect.

From still another point of view—that of versatility with regard to genre—Bonner again outshines many of her better-known contemporaries. Whereas Harte excelled in the short story and James in the longer prose narrative, Bonner was equally at home with the literary short story, the novel, and the juvenile short story. While most of her reviewers were loudest in their praise of her longer works, recent criticism has begun to grant to Bonner the recognition that is rightfully hers in the realm of short fiction. As L. Moody Simms, Jr., has stated in *Notes on Mississippi Writers* (Spring, 1968) after he has noted her arrival in Boston and her friendship with Nahum Capen and Longfellow, "Turning for material to the section of the country she knew best, Miss Bonner soon produced a series of 'Gran'mammy Stories,' in which she anticipated Irwin Russell's more brilliant achievements in Negro dialect. In 1878 she expounded the theme of sectional reconciliation in her novel of Reconstruction, *Like Unto Like.*" Simms then adds that her Realistic stories, ". . . many in dialect, dealing with Tennessee mountain life and the 'Egypt' district of Illinois," anticipated the Realism of the next several decades of American Literature.[15]

Professor Robert C. Pierle, in attempting to account for the fact that Bonner's work was largely ignored during the first half of the twentieth century, proposes the interesting thesis that, ironically, her close relationship with Longfellow doomed her works to relative obscurity following the deaths of both Bonner and Longfellow. In writing of the critical reception accorded *Like Unto Like*, Pierle notes that, ". . . since that time, *Like Unto Like* has failed to attract a single champion."

This great disparity between the initial assessments of the novel and those which followed is difficult to account for simply on the basis of a shift, however dramatic, in taste. There must be some other, additional explanation, and it may be that this explanation is to be found in the person of Mr. Longfellow. It should be remembered that in 1878 the reknowned poet was at the height of his influence; he was a living monument to the romantic movement in America, and the rising tide of change was still a few years away. . . . Thus the name of Sherwood Bonner was tied rather irrevocably to an unfashionable movement in American Literature.[16]

In praising Bonner's originality and contributions, however, Pierle at the same time recognizes the reality, the vividness, and the credible characters of *Like Unto Like;* and he recalls that "the reviews of the period were unanimous in their praise; the critic of the Boston *Courier*, for example, professed himself unable to find anything negative to say about the book and compared its young authoress to George Eliot."[17] Professor Pierle also notes the strength of Bonner's short fiction: "As she matured, however, the whole thrust of her fiction began to change, and by 1880 she was writing stories like 'A

Volcanic Interlude,' which in its generally realistic handling of miscegenation and illegitimacy does indeed . . . 'Approach the early
naturalism of Crane and Dreiser.' "[18]

The most recent, and one of the longer, assessments of Bonner's
work and importance appears in the introductory essay by Jean
Nosser Biglane in her "Sherwood Bonner: A Bibliography of Primary and Secondary Materials." Mrs. Biglane, after commenting
favorably about the vivid natural descriptions, the excellence of
character portrayal, and the humor of Bonner's short fiction writes
that "Some of Bonner's stories . . . were more realistic than was
usually characteristic for local color. Her 'From '60 to '65' was a
description of the Civil War years in the South—a description realistic in its pathos and uncolored by sentimental lamentations. Also
harshly realistic were her accounts of the Yellow Fever epidemic in
'The Yellow Plague of '78: A Record of Horror and Heroism' and in
'The Revolution in the Life of Mr. Balingall.' "[19] Mrs. Biglane's final
commentary suggests the importance of a study of Bonner's work to
the literary critic and historian of today: "Sherwood Bonner's literary importance lies in the fact that not only was she one of the first to
write in the local-color genre that was not wide-spread until the
1880's, but also in the fact that she was one of the first post-war
Southerners to reject the idea of Southerners writing for the purpose of a Southern literature and to promote, instead, the movement of Southerners writing for an American literature."[20]

As a final comment about Bonner's work, one should not overlook
her very obvious talent as a writer of humor. Whether it is the
humor of dialect under the influence of the Southwest humorists or
the humor of ironic and incongruous plot, Bonner is an amusing and
gifted author. She had a way of using words and for giving the right
speech to the right character at the right moment. Her
"Gran'mammy" tales read well even today, and her political satire in
Like Unto Like is as topical today as it was during the Gilded Age.
The result of her combination of all of these attributes is that Sherwood Bonner has a permanent corner in American literature as a
transitional writer who helped, along with numerous other minor
writers, to prepare the American public for the advent in just a few
short years of Realism and Naturalism.

Notes and References

Preface

1. Max Herzberg, *Reader's Encyclopedia of American Literature* (New York, 1962), p. 432.
2. Edward Wagenknecht, *Longfellow: A Full-length Portrait* (New York, 1955), p. 280.
3. Claude M. Simpson, ed., *The Local Colorists* (New York, 1960), p. 289.

Chapter One

1. Nash Kerr Burger, "Katherine Sherwood Bonner: A Study in the Development of a Southern Literature," M.A. thesis, University of Virginia, 1935, p. 15.
2. Dorothy Gilligan, "The Life and Works of Sherwood Bonner," M.A. thesis, George Washington University, 1930, pp. 1, 2.
3. Burger, p. 20.
4. George Stephenson, "Sherwood Bonner, Life and Letters," undated and unpublished personal paper, p. 3.
5. Ibid.
6. Ibid., p. 4.
7. Burger, p. 20.
8. Records, Christ Church, Holly Springs, Mississippi.
9. Stephenson, p. 3.
10. Information from a conversation with Dr. George Stephenson, April 17, 1963.
11. Alexander L. Bondurant, *Sherwood Bonner–Her Life and Place in the Literature of the South* (Jackson, Mississippi: Mississippi Historical Society, 1899), p. 44
12. *Suwanee River Tales* (Boston, 1884), p. 24.
13. Stephenson, conversation, March 15, 1963.
14. Ibid.
15. *Suwanee River Tales*, p. iv.
16. William Baskerville Hamilton, "Holly Springs, Mississippi, to the Year 1878," M.A. thesis, University of Mississippi, 1931, pp. 39–40.

17. Ibid.
18. Ibid., p. 2.
19. Ibid., pp. 2, 20–21.
20. Ibid., p. 44.
21. Ibid., p. 110.
22. Stephenson, p. 4.
23. Hamilton, p. 8.
24. Ibid., p. 110.
25. Ibid., p. 111.
26. Ibid.
27. Ibid., pp. 119–20.
28. Ibid., pp. 126–27.
29. Ibid., pp. 117–18.
30. Ibid., p. 123.
31. Ibid., pp. 124–25.
32. Ibid., p. 15.
33. Ibid., p. 22.
34. Bonner's personal diary for 1869; possessed by Mr. David McDowell, Batesville, Mississippi.
35. Hamilton, p. 11.
36. Bonner's diary, passim.
37. Hamilton, pp. 228–29.
38. Stephenson, p. 4.
39. Bondurant, p. 45.
40. *Suwanee River Tales*, p. 4.
41. Ibid., p. 5.
42. Jay B. Hubbell, *The South in American Literature 1607–1900* (Durham, 1954), pp. 357–58.
43. *Like Unto Like* (1878), p. 17.
44. Burger, pp. 27–28.
45. Ibid., p. 29.
46. Ibid.
47. Stephenson, p. 5.
48. Ibid.
49. *Like Unto Like*, p. 39.
50. Hamilton, p. 158.
51. Stephenson, p. 4.
52. Stephenson, p. 5.
53. *Like Unto Like*, pp. 38–39.
54. Mrs. N. D. Deupree, *Some Historic Homes in Mississippi*, no date or place of publication.
55. "From '60 to '65," *Lippincott's Magazine* 18 (October, 1876), 502.
56. Ibid.
57. Ibid., p. 502.

58. Ibid., p. 503.
59. Ibid., pp. 503–4.
60. Gilligan, p. 10.
61. "From '60 to '65," p. 504.
62. Hamilton, pp. 57–58.
63. "From '60 to '65," pp. 504–5.
64. Ibid., p. 505.
65. Ibid.
66. Stephenson, conversation, March 15, 1963.
67. Ibid.
68. "From '60 to '65," p. 505.
69. Ibid.
70. Ibid.
71. Hamilton, p. 70.
72. Ibid., p. 47, and *Like Unto Like*, passim.
73. *Like Unto Like*, p. 124.
74. "From '60 to '65," p. 506.
75. Ibid., p. 507.
76. Ibid., p. 508.
77. Records, Christ Church, Holly Springs, Mississippi.
78. Stephenson, conversation, March 15, 1963.
79. Burger, p. 31.
80. *Suwanee River Tales*, p. 193.
81. Ibid., pp. 37–38.
82. "From '60 to '65," p. 508.
83. Ibid.
84. Ibid., p. 509.
85. Ibid.
86. Ibid.
87. Stephenson, p. 6.
88. Bonner, *Suwanee River Tales*, p. 5.
89. Burger, p. 32.
90. Bondurant, p. 47.
91. *Suwanee River Tales*, p. 50.
92. "From '60 to '65," p. 506.
93. Ibid., p. 507.
94. Hamilton, p. 62.
95. Bondurant, p. 47.
96. Information from a conversation with David McDowell, Batesville, Mississippi, May 26, 1963.
97. Bonner's diary, January 20, 1869.
98. Ibid., May 12.
99. Ibid., July 4.
100. *Like Unto Like*, p. 38.

101. Bonner's diary, March 1, 1869.
102. *Like Unto Like*, p. 98.
103. Bonner, diary, September 26, 1869.
104. Ibid., October 15, 1869.
105. Ibid., December 26, 1869.

Chapter Two

1. Records, Christ Church, *Marriages*, I, 233.
2. Stephenson, p. 5.
3. Records, Supreme Court, State of Mississippi, docket number 4760, March 30, 1885, as filed in Chancery Court, Marshall County, Holly Springs, Mississippi.
4. Stephenson, p. 5.
5. Ibid., pp. 5–6.
6. Records, Marshall County Chancery Court, July Term, 1883, items number 1650 through 1657.
7. *Suwanee River Tales*, p. iv.
8. Stephenson, p. 5.
9. Longfellow Collection, Houghton Library, Harvard University.
10. *Suwanee River Tales*, p. iv.
11. Longfellow Collection, Houghton Library, Harvard University.
12. Stephenson, p. 7.
13. Longfellow Collection, Houghton Library, Harvard University.
14. Burger, p. 57.
15. William Malone Baskerville, *Southern Writers: Biographical and Critical Studies* (Nashville, 1903), pp. 94–95.
16. Gilligan, p. 20.
17. Ibid., p. 14.
18. Ibid., p. 21.
19. Stephenson, p. 10.
20. Gilligan, p. 22.
21. Stephenson, p. 8.
22. Longfellow Collection, Houghton Library, Harvard University.
23. Gilligan, pp. 26–27.
24. Max Herzberg, *The Reader's Encyclopedia of American Literature* (New York, 1962), p. 674.
25. This letter is reproduced from a copy of the original letter furnished to the Mississippi Department of Archives by Mrs. N. Fant Thompson of Holly Springs, Mississippi.
26. Longfellow Collection, Houghton Library, Harvard University.
27. "Our Letter From Rome: Peculiarities of Sight Seers [*sic*]—Farewell Visits," Memphis *Avalanche*, June 18, 1876, p. 1.
28. Burger, p. 62.
29. Longfellow Collection, Houghton Library, Harvard University.

30. Stephenson, pp. 63–64.
31. Ibid., p. 14.
32. *Suwanee River Tales*, p. iv.
33. This letter is reproduced from a photostat copy of the original letter located in the Manuscript Department at Duke University Library.
34. Longfellow Collection, Houghton Library, Harvard University.
35. Burger, p. 65.
36. Longfellow Collection, Houghton Library, Harvard University.
37. Longfellow Collection, Houghton Library, Harvard University. (March 7, 1878).
38. Ibid.
39. Burger, pp. 74–75.
40. Hamilton, pp. 82, 85.
41. Stephenson, p. 16.
42. "A Chapter in the History of the Epidemic of 1878," Press of the McComb City Weekly *Intelligencer*, 1879, pp. 8–9, 12.
43. Bonner, *Suwanee River Tales*, p. vii.
44. Letter from Sherwood Bonner to Henry W. Longfellow Collection, Houghton Library, Harvard University. (May 1, 1879).
45. Longfellow Collection, Houghton Library, Harvard University. (August 12, 1879).
46. Longfellow Collection, Houghton Library, Harvard University. (December 8, 1879).
47. Records, Marshall County Chancery Court.
48. Ibid.
49. Ibid.
50. *Suwanee River Tales*, p. vii.
51. Records, Marshall County Chancery Court.
52. Longfellow Collection, Houghton Library, Harvard University.
53. Edward Wagenknecht, *Longfellow: A Full-Length Portrait* (New York, 1955), p. 282.
54. Stephenson, p. 19.
55. Records, Marshall County Chancery Court.
56. Baskerville, p. 108.
57. *Suwanee River Tales*, p. iii.
58. Records, Marshall County Chancery Court.
59. Ibid.
60. Baskerville, pp. 109–10.
61. *Suwanee River Tales*, p. viii.

Chapter Three

1. Sherwood Bonner, *Dialect Tales* (New York, 1883), p. 35.
2. Ibid., p. 24.
3. Ibid., pp. 53–54.

4. Ibid., pp. 57–58.
5. Ibid., pp. 81–82.
6. Ibid., p. 90.
7. Ibid., pp. 94–95.
8. Ibid., pp. 100–1.
9. Ibid., p. 121.
10. Ibid., pp. 125–26.
11. Ibid., p. 133.
12. Ibid., pp. 149–50.
13. Ibid., p. 166.

Chapter Four

1. Bonner, *Suwanee River Tales*, p. iv.
2. Herzberg, p. 432.
3. Bondurant, p. 55.
4. Twain, *Huck Finn*, p. xx.
5. *Suwanee River Tales*, p. 4.
6. Ibid., p. 5.
7. Ibid., p. 6.
8. Ibid., p. 13.
9. Ibid., pp. 11–12.
10. Ibid., pp. 16–17.
11. Ibid., p. 30.
12. Ibid., pp. 31–32.
13. Ibid., pp. 36–37.
14. Ibid., p. 40.
15. Ibid., pp. 44–45.
16. Ibid., pp. 55–56.
17. Ibid., p. vii.
18. Ibid., pp. 132–33.
19. Ibid., p. 178.
20. Biglane, "Sherwood Bonner: A Bibliography of Primary and Secondary Materials," p. 43.

Chapter Five

1. Claude M. Simpson, ed., *The Local Colorists* (New York, 1960), p. 289.
2. Ibid., p. 300.
3. Ibid., pp. 301–3.
4. Ibid., p. 292.
5. Ibid., p. 289.

Chapter Six

1. "The Valcours," pp. 243–44.
2. *Like Unto Like*, p. v.

3. Ibid., p. 16.
4. Ibid., p. 13.
5. Ibid., p. 63.
6. Ibid., p. 86.
7. Ibid., p. 145.
8. Ibid., p. 117.
9. Ibid., p. 102.
10. Ibid., p. 95.
11. Ibid., p. 25.
12. Ibid., p. 47.
13. Ibid., p. 44.
14. Ibid., p. 136.
15. Ibid., p. 163.
16. Ibid., pp. 163–64.
17. Ibid., p. 169.
18. Ibid., pp. 168–69.
19. Ibid., p. 148.
20. Ibid., p. 149.
21. Ibid., p. 127.
22. Ibid., p. 163.
23. Ibid., p. 76.
24. Ibid., p. 146.
25. Ibid., p. 60–61.
26. Ibid., p. 159.
27. Ibid., p. 169.
28. Burger, p. 76.
29. Burger, p. 75.
30. Burger, p. 83.
31. Burger, p. 87.
32. Oscar Fay Adams, *A Dictionary of American Authors* (Cambridge, 1898), pp. 241–42.
33. Records, Marshall County Chancery Court.
34. Ibid.
35. *Suwanee River Tales*, p. vi.
36. Ellen W. Kirk, *The Story of Margaret Kent* (Boston, 1886), p. 41.
37. Ibid., p. 32.
38. Ibid., pp. 367–68.
39. Ibid., pp. 361–62.
40. Ibid., pp. 197–98.
41. Ibid., pp. 33–34.
42. Ibid., p. 36.
43. Ibid., p. 64.
44. McDowell, conversation, May 26, 1963.
45. *Suwanee River Tales*, p. vii.
46. Kirk, p. 301.

47. Ibid., p. 60.

48. Anon., "Sherwood Bonner," *Harper's Weekly* 27 (August 11, 1883), 503.

49. *Like Unto Like*, p. 76.

Chapter Seven

1. Paul Hamilton Hayne, a review of *Like Unto Like*, Louisville Sunday *Argus*, November 17, 1878.

2. Ibid.

3. R. W. Knott, "Southern Literature," Louisville *Argus*, no date. (A copy of this review is in the possession of David McDowell, Batesville, Mississippi; the article, a reply to Hayne, probably appeared four to six weeks later.)

4. Unsigned review of *Like Unto Like*, Boston *Advertiser*, February 9, 1879.

5. Unsigned review of *Like Unto Like*, Portland *Press*, October 5, 1878.

6. Unsigned review of *Like Unto Like*, St. John, New Brunswick *Globe*, October 16, 1878.

7. Unsigned review of *Like Unto Like*, Boston *Courier*, October 20, 1878.

8. Ibid.

9. Baskerville, *Southern Writers*, p. v.

10. Ibid., p. 107.

11. Ibid., p. 115.

12. Ibid., p. 118.

13. Bondurant, p. 56.

14. Wagenknecht, *Longfellow: A Full-Length Portrait*, p. 280.

15. Simms, p. 25.

16. Pierle, pp. 20–21.

17. Ibid., p. 19.

18. Ibid., p. 21.

19. Biglane, p. 44.

20. Idem.

Selected Bibliography

PRIMARY SOURCES

1. Travel Articles

"At Venice: Sherwood Bonner Visits the 'Bride of the Sea' and Is Happy," Memphis *Avalanche*, August 6, 1876, p. 1.

"Beautiful Florence: The Art Galleries of the Birthplace of Michaelangelo," Memphis *Avalanche*, July 9, 1876, p. 2.

"The Big Celebration: An *Avalanche* Correspondent's Impressions of the Lexington-Concord Centennial," Memphis *Avalanche*, May 4, 1875, p. 2.

"Boston's Centennial: A Southern Woman's Description of the Celebration at Bunker Hill," Memphis *Avalanche*, June 30, 1875, p. 2.

"Our Letter From Rome: Peculiarities of Sight Seers [*sic*]—Farewell Visits," Memphis *Avalanche*, June 18, 1876, p. 1.

"Rome's Carnival: Sherwood Bonner's Description of Carnival Week in the Eternal City," Memphis *Avalanche*, April 9, 1876, p. 2.

"Sherwood Bonner's Letter: Longfellow's Home—Its History," Memphis *Avalanche*, December 26, 1875, p. 2.

"Sherwood Bonner: A Southern Woman's Impressions of England and the English," Memphis *Avalanche*, March 15, 1876, p. 1.

"Sherwood Bonner: A Southern Woman's Trip from London to Rome," Memphis *Avalanche*, February 22, 1876, p. 1.

"Sherwood Bonner: An *Avalanche* Correspondent's Visit to the Pope," Memphis *Avalanche*, April 30, 1876, p. 2.

"Sherwood Bonner: A Picture of Social Life in the Eternal City," Memphis *Avalanche*, May 14, 1876, p. 1.

"Sherwood Bonner: A Charming Web of Italian Gossip—Visiting Garibaldi—Victor Emmanuel's Superstition," Memphis *Avalanche*, May 28, 1876, p. 2.

"Wendell Phillips: Interviewed by a Southern Girl," Memphis, Tennessee *Avalanche*, May 30, 1875, p. 2.

2. Fiction and Poetry

"The Angel in the Lilly Family," *Harper's Young People* 1 (October 19, 1880), 756–57.

"A Chapter in the History of the Epidemic of 1878," Press of the McComb
    City Weekly *Intelligencer*, McComb City, Mississippi, 1879.
"Christmas Eve at Tuckyho," *Lippincott's Magazine* 33 (January, 1884),
    51–65.
Dialect Tales. New York: Harper & Brothers, 1883.
"From '60 to '65," *Lippincott's Magazine* 18 (October, 1876), 500–9.
Like Unto Like. New York: Harper & Brothers, 1878.
"Miss Willard's Two Rings," *Lippincott's Magazine* 16 (December, 1875),
    754–61.
"Pages of Poems," *Harper's Young People* 1 (September 7, 1880), 661.
"Pages of Poems," *Harper's Young People* 1 (October 12, 1880), 741.
Suwanee River Tales. Boston: Roberts Brothers, 1884.
"The Valcours," *Lippincott's Magazine* 27 (September, 1881), 243–58; (Oc-
    tober, 1881), 345–61; (December, 1881), 555–70.
"The Yellow Plague of '78: A Record of Horror and Heroism," *The Youth's
    Companion* 52 (April 3, 1879), 117–19.
3. Unpublished Materials
Chancery Court Records, Marshall County, Mississippi. July Term, 1883,
    items numbered 1650 through 1657. Legal documents relating to the
    custody of Sherwood Bonner's daughter, her will, etc.
Christ Church, Holly Springs, Mississippi. *Baptisms*, vol. I, p. 98. Mar-
    riages, vol. I, p. 233. Records used to establish the validity of dates
    contradicted by earlier biographers.
H. W. Longfellow to Sherwood Bonner, dated February 27, 1876. Actually
    a copy of a letter mentioned by several biographers currently in the
    State Department of Archives, Jackson, Mississippi. (The original has
    never been found, nor have the other letters written from Longfellow
    to Bonner, although in her letters to him there are repeated and
    specific references to such letters.)
Sherwood Bonner to H. W. Longfellow. There are fifty-four such letters in
    the Longfellow Collection, Houghton Library, Harvard University.

SECONDARY SOURCES

ADAMS, OSCAR FAY. *A Dictionary of American Authors*. Cambridge, Mas-
    sachusetts: n.p., 1898. Early directory of major and minor American
    authors; cursory but helpful, especially about relatively obscure
    figures.
BASKERVILLE, WILLIAM MALONE. ed., *Southern Writers: Biographical and
    Critical Studies*. Nashville: n.p., 1903. Pamphlet size, largely bio-
    graphical introduction to nineteenth-century Southern authors.
BIGLANE, JEAN NOSSER. "An Annotated and Indexed Edition of the Letters
    of Sherwood Bonner (Catherine Sherwood Bonner McDowell)." Un-
    published Master's thesis, Mississippi State University, 1972. Helpful

and convenient, for letters are much easier to study than in microfilm version.

————. "Sherwood Bonner: A Bibliography of Primary and Secondary Materials." *American Literary Realism: 1870–1910*, vol. 5, no. 1 (Winter, 1972), pp. 39–60. Not only the most complete bibliography to date, the article also contains an excellent introduction to Bonner and her principal writings.

BONDURANT, ALEXANDER L. *Sherwood Bonner: Her Life and Place in the Literature of the South.* Published by the Mississippi Historical Society, 1899, in Jackson, Mississippi. Preliminary estimate of Bonner's position, with little attention paid to the individual stories.

BURGER, NASH KERR. "Katherine Sherwood Bonner: A Study in the Development of a Southern Literature." Master's thesis, University of Virginia, 1935. Extremely useful, because Burger had access to family papers no longer available.

FRANK, WILLIAM L. "Sherwood Bonner's Diary for the Year 1869." *Notes on Mississippi Writers* 3 (Winter, 1971), 111–30; 4 (Spring, 1971), 22–40; 4 (Fall, 1971), 64–83. A brief biographical introduction to Bonner, together with an annotated printing of the only known diary of Sherwood Bonner.

GILLIGAN, DOROTHY. "The Life and Works of Sherwood Bonner." Master's thesis, George Washington University, 1930. Helpful as general introduction to Bonner's contributions.

HAMILTON, W. B. "Holly Springs." Master's Thesis, University of Mississippi, 1931. Useful statistics for background material.

HAMMOND, LILIAN KIRK. "Sunday in Tippah." *Atlantic Monthly* 109 (February, 1912), 206–10. This and the following two articles, written by a family friend of Sherwood Bonner, portray life in Holly Springs, Mississippi, and Bonner's home as it existed twenty-five years ago; helpful only for background information.

————. "The Tippah Philharmonic." *Atlantic Monthly* 109 (January, 1912), 80–83.

————. "The Young Women of Timmah." *Atlantic Monthly* 108 (December, 1911), 843–47.

HARRIS, JOEL CHANDLER, ed., *et al. Library of Southern Literature.* Atlanta: n.p., 1907. Anthology of short fiction, consisting primarily of local-color stories.

HERZBERG, MAX J. *The Reader's Encyclopedia of American Literature.* New York: Crowell Publishing Co., 1962. Biographical and critical sketches of minor and major authors; entries about major figures are signed brief articles.

HOLLIDAY, CARL. *A History of Southern Literature.* New York: The Neale Publishing Co., 1906. Early attempt to create a separate genre for Southern literature.

JONES, JOSEPH. *et al. American Literary Manuscripts.* Austin: The University of Texas Press, 1960. Checklist of library holdings in the United States, compiled under the auspices of the Modern Language Association of America.

KIRK, ELLEN W. *The Story of Margaret Kent.* Boston: Ticknor and Company, 1886. Because of the close relationship of the author with Sherwood Bonner and because the plot outlines follow very closely Bonner's life, many readers and some critics believe this novel is actually a biography of Sherwood Bonner, possibly begun by Bonner and completed by Kirk after Bonner's death.

PIERLE, ROBERT C. "Sherwood Who? A Study in the Vagaries of Literary Evaluation." *Notes on Mississippi Writers* 2 (Spring, 1969), 18–22. A brief article that attempts to account for Bonner's relative obscurity after her initial work had been so well received.

"Sherwood Bonner." *Harper's Weekly* 27 (August 11, 1883), 503. A brief and unsigned tribute to Bonner, lamenting the fact that her early death prevented her from realizing her potential.

SIMMS, L. MOODY, JR. "Sherwood Bonner: A Contemporary Appreciation." *Notes on Mississippi Writers* 2 (Spring, 1968), 25–33. A brief biographical summary, together with a reprinting of an anonymous tribute to Bonner that appeared in *Harper's Weekly,* August 11, 1883.

SIMPSON, CLAUDE M., ed., *The Local Colorists.* New York: Harper and Brothers, 1960. An anthology of short fiction with an emphasis on the contributions to literary realism on the part of the local-color writers.

STEVENSON, GEORGE R. "Sherwood Bonner, Life and Letters." An undated and unpublished family paper in possession of Dr. Stephenson; a brief, informal essay. A highly readable account, containing family anecdotes and personal recollections.

WAGENKNECHT, EDWARD. *Longfellow: A Full-Length Portrait.* New York: Longman, Green, 1955. Interesting for its discussion of the relationship that existed between the poet and Bonner.

WATKINS, KATHERINE VIRGINIA. "Sherwood Bonner." Master's thesis, University of Mississippi, 1963. Adds no new material not available earlier.

Index

157